The Erastist

Michael Kessler

Dedicated to Everyone

Who Helped Create

The Constitutional, Global Civilization

Table of Contents

Introduction

Since 1977, I have been pursuing a world peace work based on a new reality paradigm, or a new model of reality, created by the science of Albert Einstein and the technology of R. Buckminster Fuller.

Our first reality paradigm was The Stone Age. That lasted for thousands of years. People saw everything as being alive with a spirit that defined what they are. That system of thought is called animism. It comes from the Latin, anima, meaning soul.

In this work, I use the scientific term ontology, the energy that makes something what it is. The idea was all life was equal. Hunters in the Stone Age often even apologized to the animal they had just killed saying it was necessary to feed their family. As we shall see, many people even today still think meat is a good source of nutrition.

The Stone Age reality paradigm was replaced by the Age of Agriculture, where reality was explained by what could be perceived by the human senses. They looked at the Earth but could only see small pieces of the planet that they were looking at and concluded they only lived on that small piece of the land. Say hello to patriotism.

The Earth appeared to be flat and standing still. In fact, people thought the Earth was the center of the Universe and everything else orbited around it: the sun, the moon and the stars, the whole Universe. This is called a two-dimensional reality, how reality appeared to our physical senses.

They looked to the east and saw the sun appear and travel across the sky and disappear in the west. Our language is still using their obsolete words "sunrise" and "sunset" as if the sun is the one moving and not us. They saw the moon rise and travel through the night sky and change its shape. They saw the stars blink in the night and rotate around the Earth.

They looked at each other and saw they had different bodies, say hello to sexism. They looked at each other and saw physical differences,

i

say hello to racism. They met people from other areas of the planet that claimed that area that they were from as their homeland, say hello to nationalism. They saw limited resources that had to be competed for, say hello to scarcity economics, capitalism and communism. They saw one another's physical changes over time, say hello to ageism. All of the languages on the planet are boxed inside these obsolete words.

This picture of reality was described by the astronomer, Ptolemy. It is called the Ptolemaic reality paradigm. It also is often called the geocentric, or Earth-centered, reality paradigm. People believed this reality paradigm to be true from the 2nd century BCE to the 16th Century CE when the work of the Polish astronomer, Nikolas Copernicus, proved the Ptolemaic reality was untrue.

Copernicus, with the aid of an invention, the telescope, and the more accurate information it provided, proved the sun was just another star with a round Earth, the other planets orbiting around it. He showed the other stars were the same, with planets orbiting them and some could have creative, intelligent, energy beings, humans, on them.

But Ptolemy's reality paradigm had achieved official recognition by scholars around the world. It even had been given religious verification by the Catholic pope. In fact, Copernicus would not have their work released until after their own death. It was a wise choice. Several people were executed for challenging the flat world reality paradigm.

Giordano Bruno, a Catholic priest, traveled around Europe teaching the new Copernican reality paradigm. They were arrested by the Church and tried for heresy, for teaching something against God's word. The Pope had even said Ptolemy's reality paradigm was true and to say anything contrary to what the Pope said was the same as saying something contrary to what God said.

So, Giordano was convicted of heresy and sentenced to death. Before their execution, Giordano was nearly whipped to death, their mouth was nailed shut and an iron mask secured to their face so they could not even utter a word. They were dragged through the town and burned to death at the stake. The Church accused Galileo of heresy too, but Galileo lied and said the Ptolemaic reality paradigm was true. They said the Earth does not move. Upon release from the trail, Galileo, on their way out of the courtroom, whispered to a friend: "But it really does!"

Both the Ptolemaic and Copernican reality paradigms are founded on physical observation, by describing reality by how it looks. It is true Copernicus gave us a more accurate description of the Universe than did Ptolemy, but it also cemented the idea in everyone's minds that the Universe is empty space with objects to be observed in order to get a true understanding of its nature.

However, Albert Einstein then introduced the proof that the Universe was not just space with objects to be observed, but it was doing something! This new reality paradigm proved to be the basis of the next, new reality that will be able to eliminate hunger, poverty, pollution and war. It offers the possibilities and opportunities from the creation of a constitutional, global civilization. The purpose of this book is to show how the eyes of the planet were opened to this new reality of possibilities and opportunities and achieved them.

There has been an information explosion unheard of in human history since the work of Einstein and systematized by R. Buckminster Fuller. From 2007 to 2017, more information was discovered than in the last 200,000 years and it is ongoing. Information breeds new studies that produce more information. It has been going on ever since humans arrived. Now we require machines to keep track of it all. We now have the information and technology to create anything we can dream.

In doing this work, I created a word, erasism, to mean love of the planet or world citizenship. It can be looked at as planetary patriotism. I decided to write a semi-autobiographical book on the life of a fictional character I call The Erastist. It is about how I thought my life's work would go.

I was able to meet some prominent people on my journeys. I have people who have influenced me to autograph my guitar, Sunshine. I actually did meet the celebrities I mention in the book and had them autograph my guitar. What developed after meeting them is mostly fictional.

In the autobiographical part of the book, I mention other key persons in my life, but I have given them different names to protect their true identity. People who are familiar with my life story will recognize who these people are, but, for the average reader, they will only be names.

Also, I have stopped using gender-based pronouns like he, him, and his and she, her, and hers. These pronouns only reinforce our identity based on our biology and one purpose of this book is to raise our identity to the ontological level, to the level of being and not body. Biological identity is a holdover from Stone Age and Ptolemaic thinking. Einstein showed the Universe is creating humans in all kinds of bodies and species. We still define ourselves by what's between our legs and not by what's between our ears, by what makes us human: our creative intelligent energy.

I have replaced these antiquated words with the third person plural pronouns they, them and their. These identify the preceding noun as a human being and will mean singular or plural based on whether or not the noun they are referring to is singular or plural.

The main aim of this book is to show that we have reached the historical point of being one people on one planet and it's time to create a constitutional, global civilization.

This book is a suggested method of how that can happen.

---Michael Kessler---

The Erastist is a companion volume to the Emmy award-winning television series and Oscar winning documentary.

Prologue

Interviewer:

"Looking back a few years, it is hard to believe that the ideal life we now enjoy on our planet was not always this way. That there was a time, some of you may remember, when widespread hunger enveloped the world. Every year, hundreds of thousands of humans, mostly children, died from lack of food and clean water.

There was a time, some of you may remember, when planetary pollution threatened all life on Earth. We were turning the land, water and air into poisons that would eventually kill us all. We were beginning to heat up the environment that would result in the death of all life on our planet.

There was a time, some of you may remember, when most of the wealth was centered into 1% of the population while the rest of humanity had to struggle for whatever they could get to survive. Most of humanity slaved their lives away in joyless jobs in the hope they would have enough saved to sustain them and their families until they died.

And there was a time, some of you may remember, when the planet was divided into artificial, independent "countries" that were continually at war with one another for some obsolete reason. Great resources were diverted into making and maintaining huge war machinery and armed forces to support the idea we were citizens of an artificial piece of the planet instead of the entire planet.

This book, the dialogue from the award-winning television series, The Erastist, is the story of one of the primary people who moved the planet to see that "countries" are not real and to the creation of the constitutional, global civilization we all now enjoy. At first, it was like moving the planet from believing the Earth is flat to the reality it is a sphere. We were in the very same place where the reality we grew up with had become obsolete and a new reality had emerged.

This work allows The Erastist to tell the story, in their own words, of how the planet was transformed from competitive, warring artificial "countries" to a constitutional, global civilization devoid of hunger, poverty, pollution and war.

We are privileged to have had the opportunity to hear how history was actually made and to hear it from one of its main creators.

We hope you enjoy this story as much as we did bringing it to you."

"United we stand, Divided we fall."
State motto
Kentucky, USA

EPISODE ONE THE BEGINNING

Interviewer:

"I have thought over and over about how to begin this interview series. It is not often that someone is able to discuss history making with someone like yourself, who was, and is, a central history making figure in one of the most important periods in the entire history of human life on this planet.

So, I finally decided to start at the beginning. That sounded logical since this is a biographical series. So, tell us for the record, about your childhood. I am particularly interested in the influences that formed who you were to become, to who you are now."

The Erastist:

"I was born at an early age. I have always wanted to say that! LOL!

I was the third of five children. With two older brothers, I seem to have been the attempt to have a daughter. My two younger sisters came a little later after me. With the brothers too old to connect with me and the sisters too young, in many ways, I grew up like an only child.

But my childhood was not very different than from anyone else's really. Except as my mother always said, that immediately after I was born, I was wide-eyed and looking around. They said I would lie in the hospital nursery and stare at everything. This evidently foreshadowed a curiosity and a love of learning that has stayed with me all my life."

Interviewer:

"All of this is just another way of saying you were born a dreamer."

The Erastist:

"I suppose so. My childhood dreams were centered on adventure from days gone by. I thought I had been born too late. I always had revelries of standing up to impossible odds and of great accomplishments. This yearning to know also helped to make me a better than average student. I was rather small physically, so sports were out. Academics gave me a basis to establish myself among my peers. My older brother was already one of the toughest athletes around, so there really was not much to concern me about being picked on.

Once I got into an argument with a friend's brother on our way home from school. I forget what we were at odds over, but I finally said that if they didn't leave me alone, I'd tell my brother on them. They did not know who my brother was and said for me to go ahead and do that.

My friend and their brother then began walking a few steps in front of me, and I saw my friend whisper something in their brother's ear. The brother stopped, turned around, came back and was very apologetic to me. I asked my friend later what they had whispered to their brother. They said they told them who my brother was. In this protective bubble and with a free imagination, my dreaming proceeded almost uninterrupted and is still on the loose!

In my childhood imagination driven reality, I wanted to go to Africa and live like Tarzan of the Apes. I spent a lot of time in trees. About a block down the street from where I lived was a large woods. And beyond that was a three-hundred-acre city park. I and my playmates would go to the woods very often. One day, I was going to climb up a grapevine, like Tarzan, into a tree, grab onto the stub if a branch, and shimmy down on another grapevine.

I reached the stub, grabbed hold of it, and reached out for the other grapevine. It was right then the stub broke loose from the tree. I fell backwards about three or four meters and crashed on the ground. When I got up, I discovered I had really injured my right hand. The fingers were all bent and knotted with a rounded protrusion like a marble stuck up under the skin in my palm at the base of my index finger. Very frightened, I ran home and was taken to the hospital.

The doctor said I had dislocated the knuckle of my index finger. They then proceeded to stretch my finger and push on the knuckle in an attempt to op it back into its socket. The doctor tried a number of times. Didn't work! The doctor said in nine out of ten injuries of this sort, the knuckle pops right back in. Looks like I had number ten. I finally had to have surgery to mend the injury. If I hadn't been able to mend that knuckle, I wouldn't have been able to play the guitar. If I wouldn't have been able to do that, I probably would not be sitting here right now.

I had another accident that almost cost me my life's dream too. I was working for my sister who owned a florist shop. While putting some boxes into an overhead storage place, the ladder I was on slipped out from under me and I crashed down onto a concrete floor and smashed my right elbow. That turned out to be the crushed head of one bone of the elbow joint, the ulna, and the ramming of the other one, the radius, up into my biceps. That required another surgery to fix. I lost some extension in my right arm, but I was still capable of playing a guitar! It seems like all of my physical injuries have been to my right arm."

Interviewer:

"We sure are thankful you survived those ordeals! Sounds like you were as normal of a child as anyone else. Tell us some more about your family."

The Erastist:

"I once heard someone say that to succeed in life all you have to do is pick your parents right. I picked as good as they get. My father worked like a slave to provide the best, most secure life for their wife and five kids. I never missed a meal, never went without.

My father also gave me my spiritual foundation. We had unending "discussions" about the differences we held on this or that concerning religion. My father was of a different religion than my mother. In order to be allowed to marry my mother, in those days, my father had to sign an oath to raise all of the children in my mother's religion. It shows just how advanced my father was and how much they loved my mom by saying yes. It would take me a long time to reach that level of understanding. The thanks my father got from me and my religious indoctrination was to become an inquisitor for their heresy. If I ever meet my father again, the first thing I'm going to do is apologize!

And my mother was just as great. They cooked, cleaned, and washed for their husband and five kids. My mother was the perfect counterbalance to my father. My father was the provider, and my mother was the nurturer. My mother remained a mainstay in my life for a considerable time. Long after my father had transitioned, we spent time together. It was during this time that I really got to know my mother as a person. Oh, "transitioned" is a word I use instead of "died". When we die, we don't end. We just transition, or go, from one level of existence to another. Life goes on. The body dies; we don't. We transition!

My mother and I had an ongoing Scrabble™ tournament for years. For the listeners who may not know about this game, the idea is to spell words built on one another. Sort of like a crossword puzzle. After eating supper, watching my mother's two favorite TV shows, which eventually also became my two favorites too, we would play a game or two.

The numbered letter tiles for the game were in an old coffee can. Now, my mother married in their teens, I think 17, and was married to my father just short of fifty years. My father was the only man my mother had ever slept with. Once my mother remarked that they did not know why I pulled out letters with high points and they just got one-pointers. I jokingly said it was just a matter of living a good, moral life. My mother immediately said: "Well, I don't know what else I can do!"

What a dear, loving Light! When we played, sometimes they would silently mouth words. I did see them on several occasions having a conversation with someone about something. Ironically, I now find myself carrying on the tradition!

With a foundation like that, it's no wonder that my family was also great. My two older brothers never beat me up or mistreated me at all. My two younger sisters were to become very important in my later life as my brothers did too. In fact, I did grow up much like an only child but with some very loving siblings."

Interviewer:

"It looks like you had a very good, loving foundation upon which to build your vision of world peace. I can see where you got your idea that we are one family on one planet. Can you think of any experience where you were turned into that direction?"

The Erastist:

"The first big step toward what would eventually propel me into the center of world peace events came in my second year of high school. I like to refer to such things as life shaping moments. You know those things that happen, and you are never quite the same again. Someone says or does something that shapes your life. In my sophomore English class, we were given the assignment to deliver a 5-minute speech on any topic. Somehow, probably by getting lost in my imaginary world of adventures and the new universe of television, I forgot all about the speech.

It was no small amount of surprise to me when the teacher, who was also a priest, called my name and said it was my turn to come to the front of the class and give my speech. As you can see, religion played an important part in my development from the start. But more of that later.

I sat in the last seat of the first row and the trip to the front of the class was like walking the last mile to my execution. The teacher/priests in my school wore a tunic that included a thick, leather belt. Students were often punished by being spanked with these belts while bending over and holding onto their ankles. Frantic thoughts of what to talk about ricocheted inside of my head.

And as it happened so many times throughout my life, there came that quiet little voice from deep within and gave me the topic that would basically become the substance of my life's work: superstition.

The speech flowed out effortlessly, and there occurred one of those life-shaping moments. The class listened with interest in their eyes and focused on me. The teacher/priest complimented the speech saying it was obviously well-prepared!

But the real importance was getting the experience of being in front of people, and they being moved by what was being said, by me! There was the distinct feeling of really contributing to the students and making a difference in their lives. It was on that day I decided to be a teacher/priest. But more about that later.

For the most part, my real life, as I have mentioned, was spent in worlds of make-believe. As at the age of five, I had become enthralled somehow by Native Americans. The original allure was to be a warrior-hunter and hunt buffalo on horseback with a bow and arrows. Later on, the spiritual relationship of these people to the Universe emerged to be the most important contribution. The lure of learning about them got me to walk a few kilometers through 12 centimeters of snow to get my first library card. The reason? To get books on Native Americans! I eventually read every book that the library had on them.

My immersion became complete one year in my early teens when my father took me to a Scout-O-Rama. This was a fair run by the old Boy Scouts of America, a precursor of today's Planetary Scouts. Since the people in those days still identified themselves by gender, this fair was directed toward young males.

In the Boy Scouts, there was a fraternity called the Order of the Arrow. It was originally made up of the elite scouts, the Eagle scouts, but it was now open to anyone. One of the committees of the Order of the Arrow was the Wawayaka Native American Dance Team. Actually, the old term "Indian" was still being used then.

The dance team was all decked out in costumes they had patterned after pictures and purchased from special mail-order stores. They drummed and sang Native American songs while they danced and yelled. It was all very exciting for me. I sat there transfixed while about twenty guys my age lived a life I had only dreamed about.

I never knew this possibility even existed, and it opened the door to adventures I never would have known otherwise. It was the first experience where new knowledge brought new possibilities and the power to create a new life. Another foundation for my life's work! For the next five years, I ate, drank, and slept this new life of dance and travel. It also was my first introduction to performing on stage. A real life-shaping moment!

The adult leader of the dance team, who was also its drummer and singer, took me and three other dance team members on a trip out West.

7

It was the first time I had been out of my home state. We went out to the Southwest and saw the Grand Canyon and the Petrified Forest. When I looked out into the Grand Canyon, I gasped. It was the first thing ever to take my breath away. Never had I experienced such open magnificence.

Then we headed north through the Grand Teton National Forest. It was some of the most beautiful geography I had ever seen. The Grand Teton Forest, Jackson Lake and the Grand Teton Mountains were unbelievable. I said when I transitioned, I wanted my body to be buried in the Grand Tetons.

Next, we went into Yellowstone National Park. It was like going to another planet. It had all kinds of geographic components. There were desert-like areas changing to forested woodlands changing to mountains of true grandeur. And of course, the volcanic components were remarkable. The hot springs all the way up to the geysers, to Old Faithful itself, truly have to be seen to be appreciated.

My turning toward a priest-style of thinking actually began in grade school when I was asked to leave the choir because I could not sing. Ironic, huh? Especially now that one of my songs is the global anthem. The choir director thought I would do better to become an altar server and assist the priests during the rituals. There I could memorize Latin responses to prayers and be in the thick of the religious ceremonies.

Once on a Sunday, when I was in New York with my scout troop, I went to church and there were no servers there to assist the priest. So, I went up and served. During communion, I was standing next to the priest who was giving the kneeling members of the congregation the unleavened bread, the host, believed to be the body of Christ. I was holding the paten, a plate with a handle to catch any crumbs from the host. One of the members turned out to be a person from my hometown church who knew me. Their mouth almost hit the floor when they recognized me. It was funny.

All this activity left no time for the other sex. In fact, I did not have, or even want to have, a social date until my last year of high school. I had decided to enter the seminary after graduation to be a teacher/priest like at my high school. Since I would take a vow of celibacy, it made little sense to pursue any relationship, particularly sexual, which would be seen as a major sin anyway.

But my parish priest, who was also my spiritual guide in those days, advised me not to stop dating. Since I had not even started dating, I thought I should take a shot at it. So, the choice of celibacy would be made clearly and without reservation. Famous last words, huh?

As it turned out, there was a person of the opposite sex who lived right across the street from me. Although sex hadn't been a priority item in my consciousness or even in there most of the time, it had not been a totally absent thought either. So, with the advice of the parish priest echoing in my ears, I asked my neighbor out for a date.

Seems there was to be a dance at their high school. They said they had to work a concession stand at the beginning of the dance but then would be free to enjoy the evening. That sounded workable and the date was made. But it was, upon entering the school, that another one of those life-shaping moments occurred, and it wiped out the priesthood and celibacy questions altogether.

My "date" introduced me to two of their classmates, Jo and Lee. When I was introduced to the second one, who of course was Lee, my first wife, the thought of what would happen between the two of us flashed into my mind. Little did I know the answer would be a three-and-a-half-year courtship, a nine-year marriage and two children with grandchildren to follow. And of course, there is the time we spent together after other marriages for both of us had come and gone. Lee is one of the chief reasons I am who I am today.

We know now there are no accidents, but, in those days, most people still held to the idea that life was a matter of chance and luck instead of the harvest of our thoughts and actions. It was soon after the beginning of the dance that I found out I had been dumped by my "date" and now was on my own. It was then that Lee walked by.

"Are you Jo or the other one?" or something like that stumbled out of my mouth. It was as if I had no choice but to say something to get Lee's attention. There had certainly been many other equally attractive, unaccompanied females that had walked by, but either because we had "accidentally" met earlier or had previously spent lifetimes together, I was moved to get Lee's attention.

9

The question began a conversation that lasted the rest of the evening and all the way walking Lee home. We really did like each other, but Lee was only in the ninth grade and was scared of me; a big, bad senior. So, when phone numbers were discussed, their answer was their family did not have a phone. But later, my appearance as a Native American dancer on television changed all of that for Lee, for our lives, and eventually for history.

We had a three-and-a-half-year courtship, as I said, falling deeper and deeper in love, and resisting the temptations of the flesh. We were both steeped in the same teachings of the same religion. The religious taboos against premarital sex were severe. On the one hand we had the normal, teen-aged, hormone-driven desire to lay hands on one another but, on the other hand, we had Hellfire and Damnation waiting for us if we did anything. I tell you it made for some interesting and frustrating dates. As comedian George Carlin put it, the Church was pushing for pain, and we were pulling for pleasure.

Finally, resistance was worn away and on one special evening, our first child, our son, Lewis, was conceived. Since we were planning to be married in a few months after I graduated from college anyway, what difference did a few months make? And I had the conscious thought that this initial experience with intercourse would cause a conception and decided to go ahead anyway. It is a memory I hold fondly that I chose that life-shaping moment!

I would like to add here that there was a dialogue at the time concerning abortion. There was no talk of aborting our newly conceived child. Many abortion supporters said the woman had control over their body and could abort a child if they chose. A woman does have control over their body but not that of the unborn child. Their control, and that of the male, is to be exercised before having the sex not after the child is conceived. Killing an unborn child is simply murder.

Fuller had shown that when the egg is fertilized, the human being is there and the body's development begins. The human life is present at conception not at birth. First, the human being is the fertilized egg, called a zygote. Then it develops into the embryo, then the fetus and then expulsion from the womb. The newborn infant is just as dependent on support after birth as much as the child in vitro, or in the womb. But the development continues. The infant becomes a toddler, then a preschooler, a kindergartener, and then an elementary student.

Around 11 or 12 years of age, it all changes. The child enters puberty and goes through all kinds of physical, emotional and psychological changes not even dreamed of, called adolescence.

Then come high school, college or employment, and being a young adult. That continues into mature adult years and then into middle age.

Then the body enters old age, which I call Puberty II. Another round of all kinds of physical, emotional and psychological changes never even dreamed of. Sometime later, the body wears out and we leave it. The human being, the creative, intelligent energy of the body, the life of the body, continues its journey. There are numerous ideas about what that journey is all about.

But now back to my story. After graduating from college, life seemed set up to run the course that everyone thought it was supposed to run. I had married my high school sweetheart, had a beautiful son and soon a daughter, Ann, received a high school teaching position and then bought a three-bedroom, brick home. All that was left now was to go higher up the social ladder.

My first experience of leading a classroom was certainly a chance to do just that. Even though I was only five years older than the students, I quickly proved myself and was appointed head of the foreign language department the next year at the ripe old age of twenty-one. But then came another life-shaping moment, one that brought me here.

The school where I was teaching was a parochial school. Every year, we had a retreat, a week where a series of programs on spirituality was conducted to assist the students in their spiritual development. I don't know how much the students got from it all, but in my third year there, I had another life-shaping moment, a real transformational experience.

One of the programs featured a young guy who had a presentation that included some talk and music. Sound familiar? In fact, they were, of course, a role model for my own performances later down the road. Anyway, they were talking about how unique we all are. They said that, not in the history of the Universe nor in the future of the Universe, there will never be another you.

11

That is how unique we all are. We are all the same creative, intelligent energy beings but express that individually. At the moment I heard those words, I got it big time. We all were made of the same creative, intelligent energy. No races, no genders, no ages. That was all physical. We have bodies, but what we are is creative, intelligent energy beings!

It was as if a force field around me fell away, and something filled me up with its presence. At the time, I identified it as Jesus. It gave me such a feeling of peace and joy. When I got home, Lee saw the difference in me, said they didn't like it and did not want to be married to it. Of course, what it was, was the awakening of the awareness of my own divinity: my own creative, intelligent energy.

We pretty much take this awareness for granted these days, but then it was just beginning in various ways and in different places. From then on, I was never the same and the rest of my life has been led from that experience."

Interviewer:

"I really like your phrase 'life-shaping moments'. It is amazing how our lives are formed in flashes of insight or input. I can see now how influencing were your early years and how your spiritual foundation was laid. In many ways, it sounds like your life was turning out just like everyone else's.

What got you directed to the life that the rest of the world knows about you? When we think of the person, The Erastist, who helped move the thinking of this planet to create a constitutional, global civilization, we seldom think of a high school teacher and a married father of two."

The Erastist:

"You might take a wild guess: it was another life shaping moment!

In the very beginning, when I thought about being a teacher, I always thought of it at the college level. All of my preparation was to become a tenured professor at some institution of higher learning. The next step for me was a return to graduate school, earn a master's degree and then a doctorate.

As it turned out my brother, Read, the one who provided me physical protection as a kid, and his wife, had just sold their house and moved into an apartment. The initial reason they said was in anticipation of a job-related move.

However, one evening, Lee and I went for a visit. During the evening's conversation, my brother said the real reason they had sold their house was to pay for a return to graduate school. What an astounding idea!

Lee and I decided to test the waters and put our house up for sale for the same reason, for a return to school and the rightful next step up the academic and social ladder.

The house sold in a week! With a pocketful of money, we found a low-cost townhouse and classes began. That was one of the happiest times of my life. I worked on campus, went to class, and even had the opportunity to teach German. That year was where I began to have the experiences that eventually became my transformational revolution. But that is getting ahead of the story.

Lee also had a brother, Thomas, who attended a university in a neighboring city about 150 kilometers away, and Lee and I, kids and all, found ourselves often on the road to hang out with younger, single students. As you might guess, there immediately began a series of life-shaping moments!

The first was music. It seems hard to imagine now that performing music has not always been a part of my life. But often the late bloomers produce the most beautiful flowers! Here we were in a dimly lit, semi-communal, student apartment house, and I heard someone sit and play songs I had heard previously only on radios and records. Music became a mystery revealed and a mystery solved. I was transfixed! It would be a year or more before a guitar would find its way to my hands, but the seed definitely was planted then.

13

The second was sex. Lee was the only female I had ever been intimate with. Before meeting them, like I said, sex was not of particular interest to me. But after meeting Lee, it became a primary interest. And being married very young, we weren't especially well-equipped to handle a marital level relationship. We would and did fight over almost anything and everything. We always had, and still do have, a genuine and deep abiding love for one another, but immaturity, the daily stresses and strains of living together, struggling to pay bills, and raising two children proved too much in the end.

Adultery seemed very innocent in the beginning. It started in graduate school. Lee and I had a conversation that our marriage could be opened to include "auxiliary" relationships. Lee didn't have especially rewarding experiences, but I found a number of willing partners after my return to teaching.

It was not because I did not love Lee and my family; it was more out of the irrepressible drive to experience sex with someone else. I loved Lee and the kids, but monogamy seemed unnecessary. With me being in competitive bodybuilding shape and especially after having had a vasectomy, my sexual appeal produced plenty of opportunity to fulfill my desires.

Ben Franklin once said something to the effect that two people can keep a secret if one of them is dead. My adultery secret eventually came to light and my marriage crashed on the rocks. Actually, it had been pretty shaky all along. The final break came one evening when Lee asked me to go out and get Lewis for supper.

I went outside and did not see Lewis but did see some of my son's playmates and asked them if they knew where Lewis was. The reply was that Lewis may have run away from home. I was astonished and asked why would Lewis do that? The playmate said that Lewis was so tired of me and Lee's fighting and of having to console Ann, who was crying and upset over the fighting.

Lewis said they were going to run away from home. At that point, I decided a good divorce was better than a bad marriage. I could bear anything, but if the marriage was causing my kids to suffer, then it had to go.

That evening, after crying my eyes out preparing to tell the kids goodbye, I sat down with them and Lee and said I was moving out. I said I did not know exactly how long it would be for, but it was necessary to stop the fighting. Lewis, only eight at the time, summed up the situation as only a child can: "I don't want you to leave but I guess anything is better than the fighting. And if you do come back, maybe it will be better."

I kissed Lee and the kids softly and left. I do wish Lee and I could have met later in life. Once, I jokingly said maybe we could reunite in our sixties. Needless to say, Lee didn't go for that.

During all of this were my teaching experiences after graduate school. My first assignment was at an inner-city junior high school. I lost three and a half kilograms of weight during the first week because of the culture shock. In those days, remember, we were still identified by the obsolete idea of race based upon skin color and the whole cultural baggage that went with that insanity. There was different slang to get used to hearing, different values to learn and respect. But it was here I learned that who we are is not a matter of artificial race, age, or gender, but a matter of what we do and say.

Jesus was right when he said it is the fruit of the tree that tells you what the tree is all about. Jesus said we could do all the things they were doing if we had the faith of a mustard seed. When you put a mustard seed into the ground, it doesn't sprout up as a rose bush or any other plant. It is true to its nature and pops up as a mustard tree so large that the birds of the air can nest in it. Jesus was only demonstrating to us, the creative, intelligent energy seeds, what we are capable of.

I was assigned to be a substitute teacher for a middle school shop class. The students were inner city youths, all boys. Thank God there weren't any females in the shop class. They can really be challenging. The students were about 13-15 years of age and had been told all their lives what to do, the correct way of how to do it, when to do it, and for how long to do it. Now they did not want anyone telling them anything!

The principal liked how I handled the class and asked if I wanted to have a permanent assignment. Since I was married with two small children at the time, I couldn't refuse. When I returned the next day, the look of surprise that came over their faces was astounding. I said I was to be their substitute teacher for the entire year.

I told them we were not going to turn the machines on. I added that I knew they respected two things: money and power, and that I was broke!

15

Still in competitive bodybuilding shape, they got the message. The former shop teacher even had a paddle made from a 2X4 board!

I turned the shop class into a study hall. I was still into Native American beadwork and often took something I was working on into class while the students worked on their lessons from other classes. They were very curious about the beading, and I told them we could make some looms from the scrap boards lying in the room. We got out the hammers, nails and boards. Right of the bat, one student nails another student's book to the worktable. Put up the hammers! Put up the nails! Put up the boards!

As it turned out, several of the students liked to play chess. Those who couldn't play chess liked to play checkers. I bought several sets of the two games. It became the goal of everyone to beat me in chess. I was a fairly active player in those days and lost only two games all year.

I also got to learn an inner-city version of checkers called checker pool. It was played like traditional checkers except for when a checker crowned a king. Then it could move like a chess bishop. For those of you not familiar with how a chess bishop moves, it can move diagonally on the color it is on for as many spaces that are open to it. All the way across the board! I got beaten several times learning that game.

After that trial by fire, I had myself transferred to an inner-city senior high school. There I taught a variety of courses like German, English, and humanities, but mostly it was history and social studies. It was originally the only high school for Afro-Americans in the county and the school that Muhammed Ali had graduated from. It was in the final years of this teaching that I ran into more life-shaping moments.

I might mention here that I also taught a course on drugs. I told the students immediately on the first day that we would only be studying drugs and not taking them. This was not a lab class! They got a laugh out of that. I liked it too!

In the drug class, we learned a lot about the history of drug usage. One of the oldest books we have is a 5,000-year-old Chinese medical book. It has marijuana in it as a medicine and as a social substance like alcohol or tobacco. There is also a folktale that the gods had a magic drink they decided to share with humanity. They sprinkled the drink onto the Earth and where the drops hit, marijuana grew. I am glad that the constitutional, global civilization decided to decriminalize the use of marijuana. I think that contributed considerably to the peace we now enjoy.

A few years before, I had read a book by Alvin Toffler called *Future Shock*. It dealt with the monumental changes being caused by the explosion of information of the Twentieth Century beginning with the work of Albert Einstein. This, of course, becomes the substance of my later career. At that time, though, it was only considered a topic of party conversation and as an elective subject for my social studies department.

There were only two people in my department who had even read the book and only one of them was willing to teach the course: me. Over the next few years, I was opened to information from audio-visual sources and class readings concerning the state of the planet and to the developments coming from all of this new information.

The students were interested in the subject too. I used to tease them that teaching teenagers' history was difficult because their time frame of history was what happened last night, what's happening tonight, and let's talk about tomorrow. But I was also having my reality transformed by the stuff we were learning. That's when teaching is the best: when you and the class are learning it together.

And I learned about the possibilities that this Twentieth Century information offered. It offered a chance to create a whole new future for the humans on this planet. It seemed that the only thing missing was people's awareness of this knowledge, its power and their spiritual will to create a constitutional, global civilization. Now we had knowledge and technology to do and have anything we wanted. The problem was our primitive way of thinking. As a teacher, I saw my job was to correct this gulf and replace it with more accurate and powerful information.

This calling gave birth to a song that covers changing our thinking and freeing ourselves from the superstitious ideas we were raised with as children. Here are the words. It's called Color Outside The Lines:

Color Outside The Lines

I

There are times in history
To leave the past behind
Retire old ways of thinking
Open new doors in our minds
Time for new answers
An' color outside the lines

II

There are times in our lives
To make up our minds
That this ain't working out
And things are not fine
Time for new answers
An' color outside the lines

Chorus:

Reality
Handed down
To you and me
Now we can have
Anything
We can dream
Build anything
To our design
Looks like it's time
T'color outside the lines

Interviewer:

"And you did an excellent job!

So, my friends, this ends the first segment of six exploring how we got here to enjoy the creative efforts of people like the Erastist.

Please tune in next week for more. Goodnight."

EPISODE TWO
Albert Einstein

"I want to know God's thoughts. The rest are details."

Albert Einstein

Interviewer:

"Your reference to our primitive thinking is obviously the core of
your work. You brought the attention of the whole <u>planet</u> to move beyond
this obsolete thinking, create a constitutional, global civilization and harvest
the opportunities and possibilities that lay in the work of Albert Einstein.

Can you elaborate more on ol' Albert?"

The Erastist:

"That's almost all of what I have been doing all these years. I
suppose there is a thing or two that I can elaborate on!
It was through reading all of Buckminster Fuller's books that I got
introduced to the importance of Einstein's work. Like most people at the
time, I knew Einstein was considered a genius, but it wasn't until I read
Fuller that I understood why Einstein was a genius.

Albert had brought forth a whole, new way of thinking that was far
superior to the way we were thinking at the time. I saw my role
immediately, as an educator, was to get this information out as quickly as
possible to as many people as possible in the shortest time as possible.
Generally, if anyone knows anything about Albert Einstein, it has to
do with their genius mind and scientific theories and discoveries. I have
covered some of this already. But essentially, Einstein moved our
relationship with the Universe by moving it from being an empty space with
objects to be observed to a system of activity. The Universe became a
technology that is doing something: creating humans.
But there was another Einstein that fewer people were aware of.
Einstein also immersed themselves into calling into question the traditions
and beliefs that formed the thinking of everyone on Earth. And, they also
proposed creating a constitutional, global civilization. I knew then, they
were for me!
I read much of Albert's writings, but I'll only introduce a few here.
First, I read their <u>The World as I See It</u>. Einstein thought that the person
who regards human life as meaningless is almost disqualified for life. We

21

exist for our fellow humans. Any class system is automatically unjust and founded on force.

Democracy, where all are respected and no one idolized, is the political ideal. Any complex endeavor, like government, requires leadership and chains of command but only based on the choices of the people. Force always attracts leaders of low morality.

Einstein held those people, who contribute the most to human existence, deserve the most of our love and support. The lived example of great and pure characters is the only thing that produces fine ideas and noble deeds.

And, they said money corrupts and that Moses, Jesus, Gandhi and others were examples of the unimportance of money. I knew that wealth, in the constitutional, global civilization, would be, as Fuller described, as plentiful as air, and that level of wealth would eliminate people being corrupted, at least by money.

Einstein said too the only way of educating was to be a lived example. The tradition-bound educators had become espousers of sovereign nationalism, scarcity-based, competitive economics, biological identity, and the other obsolete, traditional systems we called reality in those days, and these systems had lost their sense of intellectual validity. Teachers had become specialist thinkers, which, for Einstein, was an academic Tower of Babel. It isolated people into narrow spheres of knowledge and degraded them to the level of a mechanical machine.

Albert said all that humanity has done to date has been done to alleviate the pain of the struggle to survive. Religions were born as humanity tried to get divine help in relieving the stress of existence. First there was the religion of fear. This sort of religion promised divine bliss if you followed the tenets of the religion and eternal torture if you didn't. That was followed by the religion of morality. This was based on the innate awareness of what is right and wrong.

Then, came the "cosmic religious feeling". This last stage eliminates dogma and the necessity of a church to embody teachings. Religion was an awakening, an experience, and not merely a list beliefs and creeds. The awakening of this "cosmic religious feeling" is the important function of art and science. A human's ethical behavior should be based on sympathy, education, and social ties.

I immediately thought that erasism, my word for loyalty to the planet, is an ideal way to embody this ideal. One people on one planet! Or even better, one family on one planet! Einstein then added the people who have advanced humanity the most were those who had attained this "cosmic religious feeling". It gave them the strength to persist despite any failure. That reminded me of my own experience of getting the "cosmic religious feeling" when I was a teacher at the parochial high school.

Einstein said in times of crisis, people are generally blind to everything not in their immediate circle of necessities. However, science did not seem to fall into that realm, as a rule, but stunted scientific inquiry would dry up any possibilities of future development. But I thought too that they would be open to hearing and pursuing something that would eliminate their crisis. Of course, that was erasism, the World Energy Network, and the constitutional, global civilization.

At first, there were few people who could see through these contemporary weaknesses and follies. Many of them lost heart when faced with human stubbornness. Only a tiny minority had an opportunity to fascinate their generation by the means of art, which holds up a mirror up to its generation. I wanted to be in that minority and reach the majority, reach the entire planet.

Einstein felt that the destiny of humanity depended increasingly on the moral forces it can generate. People tried to minimize war by reducing armaments and restrictive rules, but all of this goes away when vital issues, like war, developed. Einstein thought that only the total repudiation of the concept of war was of any use.

Real people were living in dread because the obsolete tradition of sovereign nationalism was being pursued at the expense of humanity's prosperity and welfare, especially in the cost of human life.

The accomplishment of such far-reaching change in the traditional systems presupposes a mighty moral effort: "a deliberate departure from deeply ingrained tradition", Einstein said. Humanity was at a parting of the ways. The new path offered us security, freedom as individuals, freedom as a society, and freedom as a planet. The continuation of the old ways of thinking offered only slavery to these obsolete traditions and/or extinction. This filled me with the resolve to commit my life to doing whatever I could to realize the new reality of this new path. Fortunately, I did get some things done.... like the constitutional, global civilization!

Einstein went on to say it is not the duty of the individual to wait and criticize. They must serve the cause by all means in their power. The fate of the world will be such as the world creates. Improvement can only come with severe struggle, but this does not include violence.

Einstein was a devoted pacifist. The committed few were up against the powerful many, who were lukewarm and/or misguided. Deliverance could only come from the people themselves. This absolutely validated my plans to reach the planet. Like the old saying goes, "If the people lead, the leaders will follow."

Interviewer:

"You certainly were a good student! I can just see your work in a completely different light, the light of Einstein's thinking.

So, what else did ol' Albert have to say?"

The Erastist:

"Next, I read Out of My Later Years. Einstein had lived through some unbelievable history and experienced several challenging times. In this book, Einstein said that religion and science are branches of the same tree. They are both directed toward ennobling human life, lifting people from the struggle for physical existence and leading them to individual freedom. Einstein felt that a passionate will for justice and truth does more for improving conditions than all of the political shrewdness.

Then Einstein turned their attention to morals and emotions. Einstein said instinct brings thought into action, and through repeated

24

performance of these actions, the actions become traditions which, in time, eventually become fetishes. Individuals surrender to elementary instincts and hedonistic gratification to these fetishes which results in insecurity, fear, and promiscuous misery. Before the establishment of the constitutional, global civilization, this was reality for nearly everyone on the planet.

This system was also evidenced in the rise of the monotheistic religions. They made the mistake of acquiring differences based on various geographical, cultural and biological reasons and thus became a source of division and conflict rather than a source of unification. Einstein added that morals are not solely in the realm of religion. They said morals are possessions of all humanity along with science and the arts. I liked the part about the arts!

This possession gives a basis for giving everyone an opportunity to develop their latent talents. This places values on differences as sources of enrichment instead of unending enmity. Albert said it all adds up to tolerance, the basis for true morality. This is the soul of my word erasism, loyalty to the planet. Tolerance for all humanity.

Einstein continued their treatise on science and religion. They said that the knowledge of what is does not directly lead to what should be. To make clear fundamental ends and values and to set them in the emotional life of the individual is, according to Einstein, the most important function of religion in the social life of humanity. I also saw it as the most important function in my desire to reach a planetary constituency and create the constitutional, global civilization.

Einstein said powerful traditions come into being through the medium of powerful personalities. They saw the traditions of the Judeo-Christians as free and responsible developments of the individual who places their powers in the service to all humanity. Einstein added that sovereign nationalism, intolerance, and economic oppression stifle the human spirit. More fuel for my fire!

Albert saw science as the means to attain the goals of religion. One of their favorite quotes of mine is "Science without religion is lame; religion without science is blind." They thought any doctrine based on superstition,

25

which Einstein called 'darkness', will lose its hold on the mind but will cause immeasurable harm to human progress.

I thought these obsolete doctrines of "countries", scarcity-based economics, and biological identity have always caused and continued to cause immeasurable harm. It was clear people had to be offered a different set of doctrines, like erasism, and you guessed it, the constitutional, global civilization!

Einstein saw education as the hope of the continuance and health of human society. They held that school was not merely a place to transfer knowledge, but a place where qualities and capabilities valuable to the common society can be developed in the individual. They said school should develop free thinking individuals who see service to the community as their highest priority.

Albert said actual performance, not compelled by fear, force or artificial authority, was the best method of learning. And Einstein did not attain a higher education. They said they loved learning but hated school. Einstein said education was "...that which remains after one has forgotten everything learned in school."

They thought the students' respect for the teacher should be based solely on the human and intellectual qualities demonstrated by the teacher. The teacher must guard against using their individual ambition to move students. Especially, their ambition must supplement the group's ambition, not deter from it. They said humanity owes its evolutionary success in part to being a social animal. I think today, Einstein would say being a social, creative, intelligent energy being, a human being.

Einstein envisioned pleasure in self-fulfilling work as the most important inducement to work. This is akin to Fuller's differences between the definitions of work and labor in an Einsteinian reality paradigm. Labor is what you have to do to survive, and work is what you want to do with your time, like artistic expression of some sort. The trick is to take humans' inherent, childlike qualities for play, creativity and recognition and combine them with socially desired activities.

I had a teacher in graduate school who said schools should be where students are knocking down the doors to get in. But most teachers are from, what Einstein called, "old schools" and did not generally have the basis to give this kind of artistic approach to education. They thought anyone attacking traditions would have to have courage to be an example by word and deed. That pretty much summarizes what I set out to do.

Then, Einstein addressed science and society. They maintained that science is to technology what idealism is to reality. They said the practical effects of science are the development of inventions to ease life, but it also makes life more complex. The best benefit was the elimination of subsistence labor. Einstein thought private ownership of the means of production weakens purchasing power.

Private ownership also devalues labor because of excessive competition. Labor unionizing struggles in the past proved Einstein right. They said private ownership carries a power beyond and greater than traditional safeguards. At the time, technology was threatening human survival, and, just as with Greek and Renaissance science, it had made our traditional thinking obsolete. That rang as clearly to me as a bell in the night. An alarm bell!

Einstein also delivered a message to the intellectuals of the time. They said Plato was one of the early persons who worked to substitute reason and prudence to the solution of human problems instead of instincts and passions. Humans had yet to develop the systems to eliminate the possibilities of war and threats of mass destruction.

They thought we must build spiritual and scientific bridges to all of the nations, which will unite them as cities and states in the past had been united into larger, political systems. In other words, it was time to create a constitutional, global civilization.

This organization of the planet would have the legal right and duty to resolve conflicts between "countries" or any groups of people. The concept of war would be abolished. Einstein saw no historical precedents to guide us and saw the intellectuals' job as providing the solutions.

I thought they were a bit short-sighted saying this. The people in the whole unification movements that created the sovereign nations, as Einstein noted, were the guides. And war was eliminated by constitutional law within the borders of the nations.

The American experience showed that people of different backgrounds can come together into a legal union. Einstein said it is the intellectuals' job to sell this unification to the planet. You might guess erasism and the creation of a constitutional, global civilization immediately sprang into my mind! And as my Dad sold cookies, I sold a new reality far superior to the one we were then struggling in.

Purely objective problems can be solved by purely rational thought. Hunger, poverty, pollution, and war were the first purely objective problems that I thought of. Einstein said behind all negotiations lay the threat of naked power and that arming for war is more likely to outweigh the talking of peace. More instinct and passion thinking!
Einstein hoped people would be found, sufficient in number and moral force, to serve as leaders from this situation to a new security founded on a world government. After reading this, I decided I would go find them. And I did!
Einstein concluded this work by saying it is the individual who must be protected. We can only call ourselves civilized when common security is seen as a common obligation of society and a common right of all humans.
That, of course, is the soul of my life's efforts."

Interviewer:

"The more you share, the more impressed I am at your research and achievement reaching your goals.

Are there any other works of Einstein you can share?"

The Erastist:

"Like I said in the beginning, I got my information for this interview from note cards I made when I read those works. But I found a number of note cards that do not have a bibliography card to identify them. I assume they are on Einstein or by Einstein, but I am not one hundred percent sure. The ideas are in agreement with Einstein's, so I think the notes are theirs, but I can't say for sure.

There is one set of note cards that are quotes of Einstein. I thought this would be a very good way to introduce more of what Einstein had to say.

Here's the first one:

"Our world faces a crisis as yet unperceived by those possessing power to make great decisions for good or evil. The unleashed power of the atom has changed everything save our modes of thinking, and thus we drift toward unparalleled catastrophe...a new type of thinking is essential if humanity is to survive and move toward higher levels."

This pretty much covered what I have been about and the total focus of my work too.

Here's another quote:

"A theory is the more impressive the greater the simplicity of its premise is, the more different kinds of things it relates, and the more extended is its area of applicability."

I think Einstein's $E=mc2$ is the perfect example of this idea. This describes my theory of erasism. The premise is simple: we are children of the Universe, one human people on one planet with one fate. It covers multiple areas such as politics, economics and social organization. And it is applicable to every human on this planet.

Another quote:

"Newton, forgive me; you found the only way which, in your age, was just about possible for a person of highest thought and creative power. The concepts you created are even today still guiding our thinking in physics although we now know that they will have to be replaced by others farther removed from the sphere of immediate experience if we aim at a profounder understanding of relationships (in the Universe)."

Basically, Einstein is saying the old ways of thinking have become obsolete and need to be replaced by others founded on superior, new knowledge unavailable at the time to Isaac Newton. The teacher self in me took Einstein's superior knowledge as the lesson plan with which to reach the planet.

Another quote:

"...the basic principles of physics are tied up with the most intricate mathematical methods...I soon learned to scent out that which was able to lead to fundamentals and to turn aside from everything else, from the multitude of things which clutter up the mind and divert it from the essential."

Clearly this attitude became the rock foundation in my attitude to pursue the work I had committed my life to. I became totally focused on the creation of the constitutional, global civilization and ignored most everything else."

Interviewer:

"I must admit you have presented a very human Albert Einstein. I think I will follow up on his readings too. I really like hearing their actual words.

Do you have any more quotes?"

The Erastist:

"I looked over the remaining note cards. They didn't contain any quotes. And since I cannot verify, they are the notes on an Einstein writing, I decided to omit them.

But I did write a song with Albert Einstein."

Interviewer:

"You did what? They have been gone since about 1955. How did you write a song with Einstein?"

The Erastist:

"My body was about 11 years-old when Einstein transitioned. But when I got into this work, I did run across a lot of their quotes as you can tell. After I began songwriting, I collected some of these quotes and made them into 2 verses and a chorus. The lyrics are Einstein's. I did the music.

I'd like to share these quotes with everyone, and I'll add some commentary afterwards. Here is the song Einstein and I wrote:

E=mc2

I

If 5% of the people work for peace
Peace will prevail.
The atom bomb changed
Everything
Except the way we think.
It is my firm conviction that
Once psychological impediments are overcome,
The solutions to the real problems
Won't be
Such a terribly difficult matter.

Chorus:
I want to know God's thoughts
The rest are details.
When I examine myself,
I come to the conclusion
That the gift of fantasy
Has meant more to me
Than my talent
For absorbing positive knowledge
I want to know God's thoughts
The rest are details.

II

Education is what remains
After you've forgotten
Everything learned in school.
I rarely think in words at all.
I do think it necessary that
We come forth
With a positive program.

A merely negative policy
Is unlikely to produce
Any positive results.

Interviewer:

"Marvelous! I love the way you were able to organize these quotes into a narrative. Can you tell us how you came to select these quotes for the song?"

The Erastist:

"You have already touched on that. The quotes do convey the narrative of the song and the essence of my work. But I would like to elaborate on them some:

"If 5% of the people work for peace
Peace will prevail."

Einstein is referring here to the 1% law in physics. If you add 1% of something to another something, like a chemical solution or a mathematical equation, it has an effect on the outcome of the process. Add 5%, and it has a determining or predictive effect. This was the proof of my idea of getting to millions, if not billions, of people around the world to act and call for the creation of the constitutional, global civilization.

I was watching the news one night and they had a story on a program in Chicago that dealt with getting street gang members able to transform their present life of violence into a new existence. The director of the program said their goal was to "let them see something they've never seen, so they can dream things they never dreamed". That became my life's goal for the planet too.

"The atom bomb changed
Everything
Except the way we think."

War had been and still was a constant factor in the interactions of the individual, sovereign "countries". Constantly throughout history, time, energy, resources and lives were poured into developing ever more destructive weapons resulting in the death of millions of people and the destruction of billions, if not trillions, of dollars in property.

But with the arrival of atomic weaponry, we entered into a completely different reality. The destructive force of an atomic bomb exceeded the artificial borders of the "countries". We now had weapons that could blow the Earth off its axis. These weapons offered no security, only extinction.

"Once psychological impediments
Are overcome,"

This, of course, spoke to the heart of my work. My whole life has been dedicated to overcoming the "psychological impediments" of sovereign nationalism, scarcity-based competitive economics, and the divisions based on biological race, gender, and age. Einstein and I are on the same page about psychological impediments!
For me, the overcoming of our "psychological impediments" came when we completed the World Energy Network and established the constitutional, global civilization. We moved from competition for scarce resources to a cooperative harvesting of the abundant resources the Universe had all around us. We truly became one people on one planet.

"The solutions to the real problems
Won't be
Such a terribly difficult matter."

After eliminating the psychological impediments, or the obsolete ways of our thinking, we would have done almost everything to solve our problems. But there still remained the practical problems of hunger, poverty, pollution and war from the effects of our obsolete thinking. The traditional political, economic and social systems ceased to be solutions of these and other problems but now became the causes of the problems.

These horrors were the primary focus after the establishment of the new constitutional, global civilization. After the ratification of the Global Constitution, World War III was declared on hunger, poverty, pollution and war. And Einstein was right; once we had a common, planetary society, it was fairly simple to organize the programs to feed the starving, to eliminate the destitution of the poor, to create Fuller's World Energy Network and end pollution, and to transform the militaries from killingry to livingry institutions, as Fuller put it. I will elaborate on this more in later episodes.

"I want to know God's thoughts
The rest are details."

I really like this quote. I think it was Spinoza who said that God may know infinitely more than we do, but what we know mathematically, we know as well as God does. That pretty much sums up Einstein's thinking and work. They sought to explain God mathematically. Einstein was totally consumed expressing the nature of the Universe mathematically. They had even been known to leave the house without any pants on because they were so engrossed in mathematical thinking. They would just forget!

"When I examine myself,
I come to the conclusion
The gift of fantasy
Has meant more to me
Than my talent
For absorbing positive knowledge."

Einstein would often imagine scenarios that would lead to deeper realizations in physics and were mathematically expressible. These realizations eventually became relativity, Einstein's historically important new reality paradigm, and the foundation of the magnificent reality the world now enjoys. Einstein not only was a committed scientist; they were also a dreamer. Their dreaming created the reality we all now enjoy.

"Education is what remains
After you've forgotten
Everything learned in school."

I think I've mentioned that Einstein said they loved learning but hated school. It's amazing they were able to accomplish so much without a formal education. But Einstein knew that most of the education in normal schools was usually forgotten. Some of the book material would stick, but most of it didn't. And then there were the personal experiences one has in school and outside of school that have as much or even more influence on our thinking than traditional education.

"I rarely think in words at all"

I think I have already covered the meaning of this quote. Einstein was a dreamer.

"I do think it necessary that
We come forth
With a positive program;"

Of course, the positive program for me was the creation of the constitutional, global civilization. It was about the most positive idea I had ever come across. The work I have done was totally focused on the necessity of this positive program. Relatively quickly, this positive program caught the attention of billions on the planet who made the constitutional, global civilization a reality. I take great satisfaction that I was able to participate in bringing this positive program to the attention of so many people, to the whole planet, to all of the erastists.

"A merely negative policy
Is unlike to produce
Any positive results"

I had a friend who thought there ought to be a news station that only reported good news. Traditional stations, in those days of course, reported only, for the most part, negative events: wars, murders, social injustices and the like. I decided to report only good news on my tours, in my books, and for public addresses.

If people knew anything about the condition of the planet, it was the bad news. Once the good news was given, the people were eager to hear more. Once they understood the magnificent future that the new technology, like the World Energy Network, offered, they were unstoppable in moving it from dream to reality.

"I want to know God's thoughts.
The rest are details."

Einstein, as we have seen, often compared science and religion. They basically thought science and religion were the opposite sides of the same coin. Religion is based on faith, that there is a better life to be had. Science has that same orientation too plus the technology to create the better life. Religion provided the dream and science provided the means to obtain it. And as Einstein said, once you know God's thoughts, the rest are details."

Interviewer:

"Yes, I can certainly see why you chose those quotes. Your comments really deepen the understanding of what you wanted to express and of Einstein's thinking. Anything else you have to say about ol' Albert?"

The Erastist:

"Only to thank them for opening my eyes to the history I am living, by instilling in me the dream of a new reality paradigm and the creation of the constitutional, global civilization.

I would like to add too, as a musician, that Einstein played the violin. They often said that when they got stuck on a problem in physics or life, they would play their violin to relax their mind and allow the thoughts to flow. I found that I have had that same experience. Music, like any creative, artistic expression, takes a person away from this reality and puts them into a reality of soulful, creative relaxation.

I'll close with a story I heard about when Einstein played violin in a quartet with some friends who were concert performers. While playing some musical piece, one of the performers stopped and said, "Albert, can't you count?""

Interviewer (laughing):

"Wonderful! Thank you again for sharing so much interesting, historically significant information.

And, to our viewers, thank you for watching. Please tune back in next week!

Goodnight!"

EPISODE THREE
R. Buckminster Fuller

"We are called to be architects of the future, not its victim."
R. Buckminster Fuller

Interviewer:

"And R. Buckminster Fuller! I know after your work, Fuller became as well-known as Einstein or any of the other leading thinkers in history. I am amazed that so few people on the planet had even heard of Fuller before you began your work.

How did you get started into Fuller's ideas?"

The Erastist:

"We have to go all the way back to the high school class I taught on Alvin Toffler's *Future Shock.* The tradition-based egg I was raised in cracked wide open when I learned of Fuller's ideas in the book and in some audio-visual materials I used in my class.

It was after I had left classroom teaching and moved to Nashville that I got started reading Bucky Fuller's works . I began with their signature work, *Operating Manual for Spaceship Earth,* and I was hooked. Fuller laid out how we were boxed up in really outdated, obsolete ideas that now threatened to kill all life on the planet.

But Fuller was even more focused on the ability of Einstein's science, and the technology it was producing, to solve all of the problems we were facing. They said that we needed a "childish", or open, view of life to think beyond these outdated, obsolete ideas in order to competently think about our new potential and possibilities.

I was sold.

Fuller said the Age of Discovery, beginning in the 15th Century, ended the concept that it was possible to know just about everything to be known. The Age of Discovery blew that concept away and opened the door to an unheard of new period of history with a new information explosion called the Renaissance, meaning being born again.

Fuller said we were living in another such age, and that we needed Neo-Renaissance people to give a comprehensive, new view of ourselves, of reality itself, to the world.

Yeah, as you might guess, I volunteered!

They continued saying that humans first learned by trial and error. There were probably people who died from learning the difference between a toadstool and a mushroom. Fuller said what we need now is design thinking, based on the sum total of information that we now know. From the information explosion of our time, we can now design and build anything we can dream.

Fuller stated it requires moving from specialized thinking to comprehensive thinking. This resulted in the development of their term synergy. Synergy is the study of the behavior of "whole systems unpredicted by separately observed behaviors of any of the system's parts." Specialized thinking focuses on the parts; design thinking, synergy, focuses on the whole system.

From a comprehensive view of anything, it becomes clear what to do about it, and now we had, and have, the knowledge and technology to do what must be done or what we want done. As we all shall see in the next episode, Einstein gave a synergetic understanding of the system, the Universe!

Fuller went on to cover the topic of wealth. They defined it as the "number of forward days for a specific number of people we are physically prepared to sustain at a physically stated time and space liberating level of metabolic and metaphysical regeneration." (I told you Fuller's language was something else!)

Basically, Fuller said now we know there is more than enough for everyone in the real Universe. Enough to make billionaires out of everyone! We can produce wealth at the same level that we have air, which indeed we did do. The old economic systems of capitalism and communism were based on a scarcity of resources and competition for these resources of the planet. Design science is based on the abundance of the Universe, now within our grasp, and on cooperation.

Now, with the Universe as our resource base and through recycling, we can operate from a foundation of abundance and make everyone on Earth materially secure. The problem was getting this across to the people of the planet.

As Fuller put it: "When it is realized by society that wealth is as much everybody's as is the air and sunlight, it no longer will be rated as a personal handout for anyone to accept a high standard of living...". The errors of amounts of resources and distribution allowances are human errors. The more exact computation by computers belied the belief that there isn't enough for everyone.

The next book of Bucky's that I read was *Utopia or Oblivion, The Prospects for Humanity*. The title pretty much says it all for me. We were in a win/lose, life/death situation. Fuller said we needed a World War II level of commitment to meet our challenges. What I liked so much about Bucky's work is that it focused on the Utopian aspect instead of the oblivion aspect that we are constantly exposed to in the popular news outlets.

Bucky started off by discussing comprehensive ephemeralization. (Isn't that a mouthful?!) It is simply doing more with less with how much material, time and energy you have. Fuller said we now have the Universe for material. And as creative, intelligent energy beings, we have eternity and infinite energy to realize a whole new reality.

One core principle is Einstein's E=mc2, which is another way of saying recycling. That is what Einstein's Universe is, a 100% efficient recycling machine. You can change something's shape, content and location, but you can't throw anything away. It's still in the Universe.
Fuller went on to say that technology survives, and thrives, in spite of the society's political ideologies. We can survive better without politics and economics than without technology. Fuller added that most of the problems we face can be solved with existing technology but don't seem to be solvable with the then existing traditional political and economic systems. That was proven after the constitutional, global civilization and the World Energy Network were created.

Fuller thought it was time to have people "see" the world, and their synergetic role, their part in the total system, see the world as it really is.

Like artists, they need to "see" everything in a totality of experience and expression. But there are few artists who have not had their comprehensive thinking smothered by specialization. Fuller said specialization thinking leads to intellectual division into specific groups like "countries", races, genders, and age. But computers now can handle the specialization and humans can be freed to express their true talent: creative, comprehensive, intelligent thinking. That cinched my vision of my part in this historical epoch.

I particularly liked what Fuller had to say about music too. They said that music had followed the frenetic growth of technology. Think of the music of the Gay Nineties up to rock'n'roll and rap. They felt that science was a pragmatic affair and thought people may be looking to music for leadership in fostering the spontaneous development of life on Earth. That really fed my desire to use music to reach people in the development of the constitutional, global civilization and the creation of the World Energy Network. And it worked and was fun!

Fuller then addressed the opportunities concerning the concept of work in a constitutional, global civilization. In the system of their time, unemployment had a negative connotation. The economic systems of capitalism and communism were both founded on the idea we live in a reality of scarce resources and have to compete for them either as individuals, social classes, or 'countries". But in the Universe that we actually inhabit, there is an infinite abundance of resources that can be harnessed for the benefit of everyone on Earth.

Fuller continued saying industry is by nature a "world" characteristic and that world citizenship would be a natural outgrowth of global industrial growth. By the time I began my work, thanks to industrial progress, we lived at the global level everywhere except between our ears.

Transportation, communication, and even disease were all global. But the industrial globalization had prepared millions, if not billions, to be receptive to the idea of being world citizens and to upgrade our political, social, and economic systems to operate at the global level. That outlined the vision and goal of my life's work completely.

Fuller thought that from plane geometry, we are taught to see things as being bound with an inside and an outside, and all humanity viewed their local, artificial piece of the planet, their country, with a fear of the other people on the other artificial pieces of the planet, their countries. And

43

again, this was reinforced by the belief in scarcity that said there was not enough to go around, and we had to operate on the survival of the fittest model. A perfect recipe for war!

But now we know there is more than enough for everyone to live comfortably. Fuller said that if performance levels of per unit of invested world resources were upgraded, then 100% of humanity could be supported with less as compared to 40% being supported by the inefficient means that were then being used. Fuller said we were faced with the necessity of re-educating all humanity as rapidly as possible to this new economic situation.

Again, I felt that was exactly where I fit in.

Fuller thought the revolutionary changes of the 20th Century occurred unobserved by most of humanity and that these changes were mostly spin-offs of weaponry development, which Fuller called "killingry". But every priority has its antipriority. Now, Fuller said, we can produce "livingry" from the knowledge we have gathered from the development of the weaponry. The systems of their day could rapidly raise the whole of humanity to the level of "haves" and ending anyone having to be in the "have-nots".

I thought that the militaries of the world should be converted from being killingry organizations to being livingry organizations. They had the personnel and equipment to get the food to the starving and lifesaving technology to the destitute. There is a quote from the Judeo-Christian Bible that the time would come when we would beat our swords into plowshares. Fuller taught us to beat our swords of military armaments into technological plowshares and eliminate hunger, poverty, pollution, and war.

The capabilities of computers could for the first time co-ordinate a scientifically informed world revolution in design concepts and developments, which Fuller called design science. Politics should play a secondary role in the supervision of the world's physical success. Politicians would still resort to war, but as I have noted, in a constitutional, global civilization, war would be abolished anyway.

Fuller correctly saw that students are more world-oriented due to television. They learn through this medium that ideologies alone cannot do the job. Industrialization can and does thrive regardless of ruling ideologies

44

as I have said. This shows that world industrialization is as necessary and inevitable as caterpillars turning into butterflies.

The nationalistic organization of politics, economics and society needed to be elevated to the global level, and it was the role of the individual citizens of the world, particularly the students, who must lead the way. More fuel for my work. This is the reason I began my work by reaching out to the universities of the planet. I'll describe more later about those tours.

I then took up Fuller's compendium *Synergetics, Explorations in the Geometry of Thinking*. Fuller said the Mind is the human faculty of discovering the "generalized operating principles" of any given set of experiences. Fuller was focused on the Universe.

By their nature, humans are creative, comprehensive, intelligent thinkers. Specialized thinking only focuses on the individual components of any set of experiences.

This is the essence of Fuller's synergy. Once you are able to deal with the known behavior of the whole system, then all of the parts become clear and also reveal unknown parts that would have to be there for the whole system to operate that way.

This is expressed in Fuller's concept of design science. With the rise of climate change and other maladies of human activity, we were challenged to create solutions not otherwise considered. One of the first signs of global warming was how the months became warmer. Where I grew up, every month had the weather of the month that followed it on the calendar, like January had the weather of February and so on. Curing this was a big selling point for the World Energy Network.

Basically, we had to learn what is really going on and how we fit into that. If we did not, then the only logical conclusion was human extinction along with countless other life forms, if not all life on this planet. The only conclusion, like Fuller said, was mass action like we did for World War II.

That gave me great solace in pursuing my goal of reaching the planet's population with the creation of the constitutional, global civilization starting with the creation of the World Energy Network.

One of the things about this work is a quote from Bucky that became a fundamental truth I employed. They said, "The artist frequently conceives of a unique pattern in their imagination before the scientist finds it objectively in nature." As a songwriting artist, I related to that very much. I knew Einstein would too.

After that, I took on Fuller's *Earth, Inc.* In the book, Fuller maintained that the Universe is technology. It alone offered humanity the opportunity to use its resources to lift everyone out of the scarcity-based, competitive morass in which we have always existed. This revelation first was envisioned by Leonardo da Vinci. Perhaps this is why Bucky has been called the da Vinci of our time.

In da Vinci's time, we only knew 11 of the 92 elements that constitute the Universe, and the level of the technology back then made global, economic emancipation infeasible. Bucky said now it is feasible. We had the knowledge, we had the technology and we had the need.

Fuller defined wealth again as the industrially organized ability to provide the most economic security to the greatest number of people without deprivation to anyone. The traditions the dilemmas of hunger, poverty, pollution and war of Fuller's time were products of a pre-industrial society.

However, it was now feasible for the first time in history to begin unlimited production, but Fuller felt this will probably be the result of more disaster. This disaster was provided by the climate changes affecting the weather of the planet. Simply put, we had to address this and other disasters or die.

Fuller then said for economic liberation to be understandable to an eager public, it had to have periodic objectives and allowances for regular readjustments to include newly acquired information and its possibilities.

In essence, Fuller said we needed short term achievements to reach long term goals.

This led me to the point of selling the World Energy Network and the creation of the constitutional, global civilization as the short term achievements to reach the long term goals of ending hunger, poverty, pollution, and war and establishing a whole new reality on Earth. Beginning with the Network, the people of the planet were able to experience, first-hand, the advantages of a constitutional, global civilization.

The last book of Fuller's that I read was *The Dymaxion World of Buckminster Fuller*. Remember, Fuller realized that Einstein had changed the understanding of the Universe from being a collection of objects to be observed to being a system of activity that we can employ to our benefit. They, as I have said, developed synergetics, the study of systems, from that basis.

Fuller repeated that the end product of mastering the Universe is society's common wealth. The 20th century brought the possibility and opportunity of unlimited production of the resources of the Universe. We now had access to unlimited wealth for everyone on the planet. The only hindrance was the naïve adherence to obsolete, economic thinking based on scarcity and competition as I said.

They maintained that an examination of nature revealed the general principles by which nature operated. Using nature's designs, the greatest ratios of strength to weight can be obtained. The lowest common, geometric denominator of nature is the tetrahedron. This is a square with lines joining the corners. If you look straight down on the Great Pyramid in Egypt, you'll get the idea. Fuller said the Universe is an energy pattern in this form.

Fuller coined the word "dymaxion" from the words dynamism, maximum and ions. Basically, it is based on synergetics, doing more with less. Fuller said he could build a house with the amount of metal that was in a car at that time. And they did. Fuller developed the dymaxion house that covers the maximum area with the least amount of construction materials.

They saw that these lightweight structures, called geodesic domes, could be air-lifted to the remotest parts of the Earth. This would end the housing shortage and give everyone a decent home to reside in. There was even a geodesic dome research building in the Antarctic in the latter part of the 20th century.

The structure of the dome is based on Fuller's architectural concept of tensegrity. This is a balance of compression and tension. This was obtained by Fuller's creation of the octet truss. This is a string of alternating tetrahedrons (four-sided pyramids) and octahedrons (eight-sided pyramids). These form a frame that gives an equal dispersion of load pressures.

Using tensegrity, structures are not limited to size. In fact, the larger the structure the stronger it is. This opened up the habitation of desolate areas of this planet, colonization of our solar system, and construction of artificial planets and moons. You and the audience might be familiar with the ball-shaped building at Epcot in Florida. That's Bucky's architecture. Instead of being a dome, it is a sphere.

Fuller also built a dymaxion car, and it was getting attention. It was a three-wheeler with the engine in the rear. A couple of rich guys from Germany came to check the car out, but while test driving it, one was killed in an automobile accident. Fuller's car was smashed into by another driver. Fuller's car never went any farther, but it did offer construction innovations that would be utilized in the future. Things like aerodynamic construction. Cars at the time were still very box like. He also introduced front wheel drive.

Another development from this new basis of thinking was the dymaxion map. I might have touched on this in a previous episode, I forget. But this map was the first to show the whole surface of the planet with nearly imperceptible distortion of shapes of sizes of land and oceans. Traditional maps had Greenland as big as South America in order to have it fit into their concept of latitude and longitude.

For the first time in history, with Fuller, we had a map that presented a single, comprehensive picture of the Earth. And when you cut it out, it forms a geodesic sphere. Fuller was the first to achieve an accurate reproduction of a three-dimensional object, in this case, the Earth, on a two-dimensional surface, the dymaxion map.

Fuller also came up with the idea, as we have discussed, of cyborg slavery, or cyborg slaves, as Fuller called them. I prefer to use the term cyborg assistants. The goal would be to provide as many cyborgs as possible to the Earth's population. Remember, the cyborgs would do the work and we would get the paychecks!

This would free humans from having to work for a living and alleviate fear and want. And, as we now know, the development of artificial intelligence, commonly called AI, made Fuller's vision a reality. Fuller saw this would a major factor in creating world peace. I did too!"

48

Interviewer:

"Well, it's no mystery now where you got your inspiration! Tell us about the books you wrote."

The Erastist:

"The music had captured the imaginations of the people who were interested in music, but I saw that there was a need to take the ideas into another format and broaden the support for the World Energy Network and the constitutional, global civilization.

It was then I began writing. So many times, people would say to me that I should put all of these ideas into a book. Finally, I wrote it all down and it soon began to reach the non-musical audiences. I had already made a name for myself. So, when the first book hit the shelves, it was quickly snatched up and bought, and I made a name for myself as an author.

The first book, *History of the Future*, was patterned after Thomas Paine's *Common Sense*. Prior to the Revolutionary War in North America, Paine laid out the commonsense reasons why the British colonies in North America should leave the British Empire and create a new nation.

Paine wrote Common Sense in January of 1776, by July of 1776, nearly every Caucasian male in the colonies had read it or had it read to them.

On July 4, 1776, Thomas Jefferson's Declaration of Independence was issued. Say hello to the birth of The United States of America.

Later, they came up with the Constitution that created a nation from the different ex-colonies, now States in the new Union, and the whole nation was now ruled by a common law which, at that time, excluded slaves. But the foundation for a constitutional, national civilization had been lain.

That was the goal of the constitutional, global civilization, to unify the separate "countries" and be ruled by common law. I've always maintained they, the patriots, and we, the erastists, were working on the same issue: ours on a global level, theirs on a national level.

The book explores the opportunities arising out of Einstein's science and Fuller's technology and the ability to create a constitutional, global civilization devoid of hunger, poverty, pollution, and war, as I have often said. Thanks to the success of my music and touring, my book became an overnight, planetary success.

After the book reached the top of all the best seller's lists on the planet and stayed there for a good while, the invitations to speak started arriving. I took a sabbatical from music to reach out to these new audiences. I had plenty of music backlogged anyway to keep the studios busy for a long time. The crowds had made touring pretty much impossible at any rate. The studio basically got all of it together for me to record my parts then they put all of their creativity into the songs, so the music did not suffer from any lack of attention from me.

And like the music, these new ideas began to grab the hearts and minds of the people who heard them. They began to organize other groups to pursue mastering this new way of thinking. Without doubt, the central focus of all these groups' activities was the construction of Bucky's World Energy Network.

I soon had multitudes of readers to add to the multitudes of music fans working on and calling for the creation of the World Energy Network. This was preparatory to working on and calling for the creation of the constitutional, global civilization.

Then I wrote *Field Notes for the Future*. It took the major ideas of the first book and had a few erastistic, synoptic paragraphs on aspects of these ideas. Then below each section, I quoted someone from history saying something that supported what I was saying. It gave me a place to share my deepest thoughts about this work. It also was very well received. I got a Pulitzer Prize and Nobel Peace Prize for it.

Next, I decided to publish the lyrics of the songs I had written by myself and with my friend, Dave, of my first group, The Shoes. I'll discuss all of that and more in another episode.

I have written so many songs that I realized I didn't have enough biological life left to record them all.

Instead, I published the songs in a book as poetry. I thought the songs in the new book, *Lyrics for the Future*, were as good as poetry as they were music lyrics. And lyrics always were the most powerful element in my music anyway. Like John Lennon said, the music is the boat that carries the words along."

Interviewer:

"You currently have another book based on this television series. The viewers can refer to it whenever they want to discuss your work, which steers me to the World Energy Network.

The World Energy Network is now taken pretty much for granted. Only a few years ago, there was no popular understanding or use of the Internet. Then it became a primary tool in tying the world into one community.

It's hard to think now of the planet without the World Energy Network which also has tied the world together into one prosperous community and restored the environment.

How did you get started on it?"

The Erastist:

"First, I would like to lay out for the audience, and future readers, the origin of the World Energy Network. Bucky said in his book, *Critical Path*, that if humanity was to survive here, it will require four essential, critical steps or paths.

The first critical path is to make a personal, go-for-broke commitment to act, to do what you can do to turn around the dilemma we are facing. Fuller said our collective reality is the sum of our individual actions... or inactions. What we do or don't do, how we live our individual lives, creates what experience as our collective reality on planet Earth. I always said: do what you can, where you can, when you can, the best you can.

I watched a couple of television shows on PBS ones that summarized the environmental dilemma that we found ourselves in. One was called *Climate Change: The Facts* and was produced and hosted by David Attenborough. I always had a high esteem for them and their work. The show began with a discussion of the rise in the Earth's temperature.

51

Attenborough said the Earth's temperature had risen 1 degree Celsius since the beginning of the Industrial Revolution that began in the early 19th Century. It was expected to rise to 1.5 degrees Celsius by 2040 or 2050. If it got to 2 degrees Celsius, life on Earth would be under a serious, extinction level threat. They added that 8% of the species on Earth, including we humans, were threatened with immediate extinction by climate change.

The results of a warming planet were great proliferation of fires, an intensification of storms, severe drought, and rising sea levels from the melting of the polar ice caps. One stunning example of the damage climate change had had is on the Great Barrier Reef off the coast of Australia. The coral looked like white chalk and very little remained alive.

Attenborough said the sea level had risen 20 centimeters in the last hundred years. Unless that was stopped, the sea level rise would be measured in meters. If the ice caps melted, the oceans would rise to the level of the arms of the Statue of Liberty. The coasts of the planet would be drastically altered and all of the planet's port cities would likely disappear.

This would cause another factor in the effects of global warming: climate refugees. These were the people whose farmland had been turned to deserts or whose society had been disrupted by rising sea water. It was forecasted that unstopped, global warming would displace millions, if not billions, of people. Where would they go and how would they survive?

I saw another show on PBS that spoke of carbon dioxide, a prominent greenhouse gas and the cause of most of the planet's global warming. A good deal of the carbon dioxide in the atmosphere was produced by fossil fuels, especially gasoline powered vehicles. It said that a gallon of gasoline had five pounds of carbon in it. If you made that into briquettes, like for barbecue cooking, the fossil fuels burned each year would make a mountain of briquettes four miles wide and a mile tall.

Carbon dioxide, CO_2, had grown steadily for over a century. The problems had become harder to solve. The show said the problems would grow until they hit their "tipping point". This is where a whole new, irreversible change starts: the non-stoppable rising of heat. It said we needed to cut the CO_2 in half by 2030 and to 0% by 2050. I must say it is so wonderful to be here now and know that we really did it!

Next, the show went on to discuss methane. It is 21% more powerful as a greenhouse gas than carbon dioxide. There were tons of it frozen in the Arctic tundra and we nearly released it all. Now that the weather has returned to its pre-CO2 condition, the methane is once again hibernating in the refrozen tundra where it will remain forever.

Then Attenborough covered the options signaling the end of CO2 pollution. I've talked already about the advantages of solar, wind, tidal and geothermal energy production which led to the World Energy Network. One person said the costs of these actions were dwarfed by the costs of the inactions Like the protest sign said, "There is no planet B".

And people started waking up and were ready for the message I was bringing. As Attenborough said, every one of us has the power to do something. I was able to give the planet something to do: create the World Energy Network and the constitutional, global civilization!

The next Attenborough documentary I watched was Extinction: The Facts. They said there has been a 60% decline in the planet's animal and plant life. In fact, the rate of extinction had surpassed the rate of natural extinction. Attenborough added that one million out of the estimated eight million species on Earth was in danger of imminent extinction. We humans were included in that one million.

A primary concern was the loss of insects. They are the foundation of a food chain for over a 1000 other species, including humans. In addition, they are major pollinators too. Most plants rely on them to reproduce. Twenty-five percent of the Earth's plant life faced extinction meant we were also facing the destruction of biodiversity.

In the past, many millions of animals were slaughtered to support the multibillion dollar meat industry. Commercial fishing had 100,000 ships raping the fish from all the oceans. When I was in Alaska, the sea otters were losing their pups to starvation because the fish they usually fed them had been eliminated and they had to feed their pups on the less nutritious fish that were left.

Next, the human factor was introduced. The show said the human population had grown from six billion in 1960 and was expected to reach over nine billion by the end of the Twenty First Century. The rich countries far exceeded the consumption levels of the poor countries. The

United States consumed seven times the amount as the poor countries and the United Kingdom five times as much.

The over three million hectares of habitat cleared for monoculture agriculture, along with climate change, was direct cause of the loss of so many plants and animals.

Another product of habitat destruction was it brought humans in contact with new animals that carried deadly viruses. The COVID-19 pandemic in 2021 was started when scientists in China came in contact with the virus from one of these animals. It rapidly spread around the world and killed millions of people, including my sister. This spread of viruses was in part due to the killing of predators which caused disease carrying prey animals like mice to multiply enormously.

Then Attenborough asked, "What to do?"

In 1992, there was a conference that produced a treaty to address the loss of biodiversity. Since it did not have the legal authority of a constitutional, global government, the existing industries, profiting from the old ways of production, resisted any action to change their work. That all ended when the constitutional, global civilization was established. It was no longer a matter of choice; now it was a matter of law.

We found out that nature, given the chance, will bounce back. For example, the mountain gorilla grew from a population of 250 to over a 1,000 in a short period of time. We learned we could surpass any difficulty if we set our minds to it. Whatever would happen, good or bad, would be the results of our decisions and actions...or inaction.

This leads us to Fuller's second path: education. Someone once asked Fuller what can one person do? Fuller replied, "Find out what's not being done and do that."

The solution to the extinction-level dilemmas confronting all of us was, for me, like a crossword puzzle. It was solvable with existing information, and you could not work on any part of the puzzle without contributing to the solution of the whole puzzle. The only question was what part of the puzzle were you going to work on? Only information and your heart could answer that. For me, it was the World Energy Network first and then, of course, the establishment of the constitutional, global civilization.

Fuller's third critical path was uniting the planet economically. Fuller created a think tank called World Game. They said if the militaries could have war games to figure out how to destroy the world, then we could have a world game to figure out how to make it a success.

In their studies, Fuller learned that the foundation of everything we call modern was based on the access to electricity. When they wrote this, nearly a billion or more people on the planet had no access to electricity. Fuller's studies revealed that when electricity was introduced to a place, hunger disappeared, population explosion stopped, and longevity increased. Provide electricity and people had the power to raise their standard of living.

A terawatt is a huge amount of energy equal to about one trillion watts. Fuller then said the planet used about 7 terawatts of energy a day. However, the Earth receives 17 terawatts everyday directly from the sun. And add to that the power from the wind, tidal, and geothermal sources, and the fossil and nuclear fuels showed up as the primitive sources of energy they were. The energy, as Einstein proved, was here, and now we had the technology to reap it. Fuller saw the main problem was the distribution of the electricity.

Most of the developed nations had already networked their territories together with transmission lines sending electricity for thousands of miles. There were also over 50 transnational link-ups too. And now, since the

technology could transmit the power over thousands of miles, that made intercontinental link-ups possible. In 1969, Fuller proposed the construction of the World Energy Network to capture this abundant energy and supply the whole planet with cheap, eventually free, clean, renewable, non-polluting electrical power.

Fuller's idea at the time was to line the seacoasts of the planet with small, tidal generators. These would have a float connected to a small generator beneath the float. As the float bobbed on the waves, it would crank the generator to create a small amount of electricity. This electricity would be fed to larger generators on shore for the production of greater, electrical power.

The Global Energy Interconnect, based in China, had developed microwaving the energy rather than constructing power lines. That transmission then could be converted to electrical power and forego power lines altogether. As we discovered, that system had to be let go because of the adverse effects it had on the environment, particularly migratory birds.

The major need was for the construction of a number of key interconnections to tie the planet into a global network. The first was a connection across the Bering Strait. This would tie the dark and light sides of the planet together. Other key connections were between North, Central and South America, and between Europe, Africa, and Asia. To complete the system, a connection was made between Europe and North America and between Africa and South America. Like the Bering Strait, this was the shortest point of connection between these continents. This transmission system would provide a global supply of cheap, eventually free, clean, renewable, non-polluting energy to the planet.

The World Energy Network provided a foundation upon which other programs could be built. The Network directly gave the power to eliminate hunger. It also gave the power to eliminate poverty. Powered by solar, wind, tidal and geothermic energy, it ended pollution and restored the health of the environment. With the fourth critical path, it eliminated war.

This fourth critical path is the one I have walked my whole professional life. This is the path leading to the creation of the constitutional, global civilization. The time had come to rise to a higher level of political identity.

The creation of a constitutional, global civilization was an idea whose time had come. War was made obsolete.

We needed to put our traditional political, economic, and social systems and war into the garbage bag of history where they belonged. The time had come to rule the planet by law. My word erasism comes in here. It was time to love and be loyal to the planet instead of an artificial piece of it. It was time for humans to become erastists, to become world citizens.

Fuller referred to us as trimtabs. They said, on an ocean going ship, the ocean's inertia is too great for the pilot to turn the rudder directly and steer the ship. Attached beneath the rudder was a smaller rudder called the trimtab. The pilot is able to turn the trimtab and it will create a current that turns the rudder which turns the ship.

Fuller said we are all trimtabs on what he called Spaceship Earth. The question was in what direction were our lives turning the rudder?"

56

Interviewer;

"Thank you for that. You certainly have a talent for putting everything into an easily understood, historical context. Please continue."

The Erastist:

"After reading almost all of Bucky's books, I came across the idea of the World Energy Network then. Like so many others, it did not fit immediately into my narrow reality. But after giving a large number of talks and seminars, I noticed that even though the audiences were moved and taken by the information, they were equally at a loss as what to do with it all. The World Energy Network provided that answer.

The World Energy Network seems all so simple now that we have it and all of its benefits. Bucky's research showed that most of the practical problems facing the planet centered around the generation and distribution of electricity. Fuller also cataloged the growth of electric network systems since the end of the Second World War. The power companies found it simpler to build connecting lines between existing power plants than to build whole new ones.

And here enters Einstein. Remember, Uncle Albert had shown that the Universe is nothing but energy. At the time, the popularly held idea was that we had to get energy from some stored substance like wood, fossil fuels and atoms. Bucky said we now had the choice to capture the power as it comes directly in from the sun, our star, and as it is employed on the planet in the forms of wind, tidal, and geothermal energy too.

The Network not only made possible the elimination of fossil and nuclear fuel use, it stopped environmental destruction, and ended poverty and war. It could do this by the near immediate elevation of everyone's standard of living and wiping out most of the reasons they were fighting.

I decided the World Energy Network would be a hands-on project that would benefit everyone on the planet. I phoned Jamie Snyder, Bucky's grandson, who was then the director of the Buckminster Fuller Institute in Los Angeles. I told him that I thought the World Energy Network was the

57

project to pursue. They told me I should get hold of Paul Matthews in San Diego. They said Paul had been working on the Network for the last four years and had founded an organization to promote the Network.

Well, I called Paul, and it turned out that they were going to be in Moscow the same time that I was going to be there. In fact, they were attending another peace conference there. Through our exchange of information, they included a letter from the head of the Soviet Academy of Sciences. With that, I was able to set up an address to the scientists of the academy that I co-delivered with Paul.

Over time, more and more people were empowered with the idea of the Network's ability to solve some very big problems. I thought there needed to be some media event to turn even larger numbers of people onto the idea."

Interviewer:

"That would be the Bering Strait Concert?"

The Erastist:

"Yes!"

Interviewer:

"How did you decide to have the event there?"

The Erastist:

"As I said, I met up with Paul in Moscow and we did some work on the World Energy Network together, mainly our address to the Soviet Academy of Sciences. Over the next few years, Paul had great success in reaching several top-ranking officials in governments and businesses. I loved the pictures of Paul and Mikhail Gorbachev together.

After I had become the most successful performing songwriter in music history, I called Paul to see if they would be interested in pulling off a musical event centered on reaching the general population of the planet with the idea of the Network. Paul thought it was an excellent idea.

I had been thinking of an event like this for a while. Remember the Live-Aid show to educate people on the fact that hunger was now a solvable problem? It reached two billion people when the population of the planet in those days was only about five billion.

I read too where that year, three out of five people on Earth had watched the world soccer finals. That was three billion people, over half of the world's population at that time. I knew that a show featuring the most successful musicians on Earth would draw that kind of audience too.

And why the Bering Strait? It was a spot where all of the land, all of Europe, Africa, Asia, along with North, Central and South America, all of the land on Earth came the closest to joining together, as it was in the far distant past.

It is only 63 or so kilometers from one shore on North America to the next shore on Asia.

The idea was to construct two stages at the farthest tips of the Bering Strait on each side of the Strait and have one hell of a show. Each stage was to present the best the world had to offer in the form of well-known artists from around the world. Of course, these shows also became showcases for artists who were not yet well-known but were given the time and space to show their art.

But I quickly decided not to construct any real stages at the Strait itself. That could not be done without harming the natural beauty we were there to protect. So, we had the shows put together with computers. I figured that if Steven Spielberg could create dinosaurs, I could create a world peace concert/media event.

We taped all of the actual shows in some of the best audio and video studios on the planet and then mixed all of that together with the shots of the Strait. It was also actually much simpler to do it that way than to transport all of the people and the supplies for construction at the actual sites themselves."

Interviewer:

"Yes, I certainly remember watching the concerts myself. When I got to the office the next day, everyone was talking about the show and the World Energy Network!"

The Erastist:

"Oh yes, after the concerts, the World Energy Network quickly became a household word. Poor Paul was swamped with requests to get more information to everyone. Thanks to the financial support of the performers and the offices of the old United Nations, they were able to create a staff of some very capable people and had the technology to organize everything like registering people as world citizens. That is one thing I always admired about Paul, their talent for empowering and enrolling people.

I thought this would be a good spot to add information about a project we started that created a global audience of immense proportions. John Lennon said he thought world peace would have to be sold. The opportunities and advantages of a constitutional, global civilization were open to everyone on the planet. The challenge was to reach enough people meaningfully to realize these opportunities and advantages.

In addition to my touring, performing music, speaking, and the Bering Strait Concert, we also came up with a program based on the six degrees of separation idea. Someone once figured out that there were six relationships between any one person on the planet and any other person on the planet. And now, with cell phones, we had for the first time in history, a planetary means of personal communication. If you had someone's phone number, you could phone or text them. We initiated the Six Degrees Project.

I had already posted a 7-minute excerpt from my documentary outlining the creation of the constitutional, global civilization on youtube.com. For the listeners and/or readers, all you had to do was to go to the youtube.com site and enter The Erastist/History of the Future and it would pop up.

The idea was to contact everyone on our phone, email, and other contact lists and ask them to watch the video. If they were in agreement with the erastistic ideas and would like to help with the creation of a constitutional, global civilization, then they would contact everyone on their phone, email and other lists to do the same. And, if those persons are in agreement with the erastistic ideas of the excerpt, ask them to phone everyone they knew and do the same.

In a relatively short amount of time, literally millions of people around the world were contacted. From that, we enrolled them into marching in support of the global civilization. This also turned them onto the Bering Strait Concert."

Interviewer:

"Speaking of enrolling people, you certainly got the support of some interesting personalities to join into the successful completion of the World Energy Network."

The Erastist:

"Oh, you mean the League of Superheroes?"

Interviewer:

"Of course! How did all of that come together?"

The Erastist:

"That was another idea I had been nurturing for several years. People needed to be shown that it was not just an airy-fairy idea that had nothing to do with the "real world" or would ever have a snowball's chance in hell of happening.

And Einstein said they thought what the world needed was an avant-garde intelligentsia to lead the planet to a better future, a future that was not just an extension of this present reality which only offered eventual extinction. The people, like Einstein and Fuller, who saw what peace offered, had a greater responsibility to see that it actually came into being, like with The Six Degrees Project.

I had always thought that some entertainers, who had the attention of large numbers of people already, had experienced what being free was like and had the artistic, creative vision to transform this planet. Remember that the world soccer finals were being seen by three out of five humans on Earth and Live-Aid got two billion people's attention.

And during the Bering Strait Concert Project, I had met a number of world personalities who were also taken with the vision of what the new constitutional, global civilization offered. Combined with the world sports heroes also lending their talents, we soon got the attention of millions of more people. It wasn't long after that the politicians started getting on board the bandwagon. It proved to me again that if the people lead, the leaders will follow.

Their additional energy made possible the realization of one of my most treasured dreams. Ever since I had gotten into the work of Einstein and Fuller, I had been drawn to space. That was one of the great things about Einstein and Fuller. Their work took us to space, or more accurately, put us into space and laid the foundation for this society we now have.

I began saying very quickly, even as far back as when I was in The Shoes, that I wanted to have the first concert on the moon. I suppose we could have done it with computers as we did the Bering Strait Concert production, but I personally wanted to go there. I just had to see the whole Earth, blue-green, wrapped in white clouds, spinning peacefully as it lazily orbited our star at about 140,000 kilometers an hour. And with no artificial "countries" imposed on it. Now, that would certainly be a life-shaping moment for sure!"

Interviewer:

"And not just for you personally. That event shifted the whole direction of history. I don't think there was anyone left on Earth who did not know what the World Energy Network was about, who you are or the awards that lay in the creation of a constitutional, global civilization. I know there has been much said and documented about the speaking tours that followed the moon concert.

Could you talk about them from your point of view how important they were and what effect they had?"

The Erastist:

"Yes, I was asked to address a number of Congresses and Parliaments around the planet. That resulted in the decision to have a global conference at the United Nations with all the heads of state.

There, I was able to present the World Energy Network directly to the leaders of almost all the "countries" at the same time.

This televised speech was the icing on the cake. The Bering Strait show reached people who were interested in music, and they tuned in. The moon concert reached the popular minds interested in space and they tuned in. The people who had read my books tuned in. The people we reached with The Six Degrees Project tuned in. The U.N. speech hit the political elite of the planet as well as the general population.

Really, the most important listeners were not in the room at all. The most important ones were those sitting around small TV's or shortwave sets in living rooms and villages all around the planet. They got to hear the news in languages they could understand. That was one of the big benefits of holding the conference at the U.N. They already had a great staff of translators.

The UN talk was the break in the log jam. After the speech, the governments of the world were swamped by the media and the demands of their people calling for the immediate construction of the World Energy Network and the constitutional, global civilization.

We even had a World Constitution based on the one drafted by the World Constitution and Parliament Association.

That constitution was amended a little at the World Constitution Conference and became the Constitution for our World Federal Union. Now the planet was joined by law based on justice: a constitutional, global civilization! I'll discuss the Constitution in greater detail in another episode."

Interviewer:

"And that led first, of course, to the United Nations' World Energy Network Treaty. Everyone seemed very surprised at the cooperation of the government leaders."

The Erastist:

"It reminded me of the 1989 peaceful revolutions in Europe. When 750,000 people went into the streets in Leipzig, demanding that the governments get on the ball, 50 years of tyranny collapsed along with the Berlin Wall."

Interviewer:

"Much like the saying by Thomas Jefferson in the American Declaration of Independence that people will suffer ills as long as they are sufferable."

The Erastist:

"Exactly, exactly. That's always been one of my favorite quotes too."

Interviewer:

"Were you surprised how fast the Network was completed?"

The Erastist:

"Yes and no. Having spent the greater part of my life working on the project, I was gratified and a bit surprised that the actual building of the World Energy Network had begun. But Einstein said that once the "psychological impediments" were overcome, the real solutions, such as the building of the World Energy Network, would be relatively simple.

I think, for me, it became real when we completed the Bering Strait intertie. It was humorous just how easy it was. Like I said, with that one connection, the dark and light sides of the planet were united. That meant we had essentially a one, non-stop flow of energy encircling the planet.

From there every "country" joined into a cooperative effort to get the Network into their backyards. It offered them immediate access to unlimited, clean power. Asia was particularly important because they were up against trashing their environment too to meet their needs. The Network became a way for them to exceed the demands they had for power and maintain their ecology at the same time.

But that can also be said for everyone else all over the world too. South America and Africa were also quick to see the saving graces of the World Energy Network. They no longer had to mow down the Amazon and the African tropical rainforests. The industrial nations were able to see the ability of it not only to maintain their standard of living but to increase it. All of this plus improving the environment! In a matter of a few years, the Earth was well on its way to the prosperous reality we are enjoying now."

Interviewer:

"Yes, I have had many talks with people who don't remember what life was like before the World Energy Network. Sometimes it's hard to get someone who's never experienced it that life used to be about earning a living instead of having it provided by superior economic, technological and political systems.

What were the first problems you wanted to go after once the Network came online and the constitutional, global civilization was here?"

The Erastist:

"Of course, the drafting and ratification of a planetary Constitution was first on the agenda. That would make the planet a legal union. But after the completion of the Network, that eventually was realized quickly. Enough people had been enrolled into creating the new, global civilization, that when it came time for the planet's people to vote on the Constitution, it was nearly unanimously ratified. People all over the world were able, thanks to cell phones, to vote on every law that affected them.

Next, the focus was put on the problems that people were suffering from. The first major concern was, of course, hunger. That insanity was taken for granted in the pre-Einstein/Fuller reality as being just the way life was. The statistics that so many grassroots organizations gathered showed that hunger was produced by actions based on incorrect information and ideas that were no longer true.

At the top of that list was meat eating. I was led into eliminating animal products from my diet when I learned how they were the main reason children were starving all over the world. In the David Attenborough PBS shows I mentioned, they said that 80% of the arable land on the planet was used to support raising animals for slaughter. If we switched to a vegetarian diet, that land could be used to grow crops to feed people and no one, especially children, would ever go hungry again.

The World Energy Network laid the foundation for prosperity. I might have mentioned it gave destitute people access to power to end their dilemma. I am glad we are having other episodes on things like how this information led by Einstein and Fuller affected old ways of thinking like nutrition and hunger.

The first goal was to make sure everyone went to bed well fed with nutritious food. Of course, we did not do it overnight, but it was done!

When enough people began to eliminate outdated ways of feeding themselves, mainly by leaving behind animal foods, we found there was a lot of vegetable food left. Most of the vegetable food grown at that time was fed to animals and not to humans. I always said animals got fattened and children got starved.

Besides the moral issue of starvation, the environmental issue of pollution, and a host of others, meat eating is also physically harmful for us. We are anatomically not structured to really eat meat. Our teeth are not the teeth of a meat eater. Our digestive system is not the digestion system of a meat eater. The strain on our bodies from digesting meat causes the body to age faster, and we carry pounds of undigested meat in our guts too.

The militaries of the world came forth with some real leadership. In the new constitutional, global society, war had been legally abolished as a means to settle disagreements. But all of the military personnel were still there. They had the necessary equipment to get the job done. They had the planes, the ships, the trucks and the people to do the work.

It seems like in no time, we were getting to the real chronic areas and began to fatten up the babies. The militaries went from making war on each other to making war on hunger and create a new reality based on abundance. They, and we, went from killingry to livingry. We really became one people on one planet. I loved it!

Like the nomadic tribes before them had to turn away from hunting, the ranchers had to turn to alternative things to do other than raising animals for slaughter. Some had made enough money off their old business to retire. Much of the land of the present day being used to grow food was once ranges to feed cattle or other livestock. Now it is an agricultural treasure to grow food for the planet. Gradually as the meat market faded into the past like other outdated industries and traditional beliefs, a new future of abundant food was born.

The World Energy Network, which you originally asked about, came into play almost immediately. So much labor was wiped out to free the people for other work that needed to be done. In time, they even found more leisure time to enjoy. Electricity made possible the running of some simple machines that eased their labor and made them more productive at the same time.

They had power to heat their homes, refrigerate their foods, pumps to bring them clean water, lights to work and read by. They began to irrigate more land where necessary and to add this bounty to end hunger on our planet. I remember the announcement of the last recorded death due to hunger. And, as usual, it was a young child.

I am tickled when I hear people who were born onto the planet after the end of hunger. They, growing up with all of this abundance, find it hard to understand how people could be so trapped in such outdated ways of thinking and even starve people to death."

Interviewer:

"Yes, I guess it's like us being told about the days of racial slavery. Racism is another of those old-fashioned ideas that you helped to end. But we'll cover those in later episodes, as you mentioned.
Now that the end of animal foods and the Network are turning the corner on hunger, how did all of that bring about the cleaning and restoration of the environment?"

The Erastist:

"The environmental destruction of the planet was the coal mine canary for the constitutional, global civilization movement. The coalminers of long ago often had a caged canary down in the mine with them. The deadly, and often explosive, gases, that sometimes were released while digging the coal, were normally colorless, odorless and fatal. The canary was more susceptible to the gases than were the miners.
If the birds were affected at all, it usually gave the miners a chance to get out of the mine alive. The environment was like that for us. It was our canary. And its succumbing to climate changes and other kinds of pollution made us get out of our traditional thinking to survive.

The Arctic began warming much faster than the rest of the planet because it was always tilted toward the sun. This began the melting of the trillions of tons of frozen methane in the permafrost. This created lakes where there once was ice. And the methane literally boiled out at over 200 million tons a day. And methane is over 20% more of a greenhouse gas than carbon dioxide.

We were so trapped inside our old ways of thinking that we could not see the effects of our backward actions or ignored them to sustain monetary profit. The air, land, and water were the canaries that got sicker. Of course, the first ones to react were the environmentalists. They began the actions that eventually resulted in the survival of humanity on this planet, and all other life too for that matter.

The main thing they did at the outset was to begin gathering information. They showed that the problems were based in the everyday actions of each one of us. It was no small surprise that animal foods came forth as one of the main ingredients in the puzzle.

Besides consuming most of the crops grown on the land that could produce vegetable foods but instead produced hunger, the production of animal foods also was one of the main things destroying our environment. For example, the chief water polluter of the old United States was animal blood. Nine million animals a day were slaughtered in the U.S. alone and millions more around the world, and the blood usually went directly into the streams and rivers.

Then there was the matter of the animals' body waste. Tons of urine and feces were dumped into the water and land daily. They were also a huge source of methane gas that accelerated global warming. Add to that the herbicides and pesticides used on the crops to feed these poor animals and, through them, were fed to us, and you have a recipe for a very sick ecology.

The concern about the environment was that the destruction was unavoidable. Regardless of the old ideas the people were using, like animal foods, the results showed up in the air, land, and water. It was imperative that we solve them because, despite the differences created by our old ideas we had, we all had to have breathable air, arable land, and clean water to survive. For the first time, we were being threatened as one people on one planet.

As I have mentioned, the "countries" were formed when the people were threatened at the national level and had to organize themselves at the national level and resist at the national level to adequately meet their common, national threat. Now, regardless of their love for their traditional identity, every single person on the planet was being threatened personally, individually, by their assaults on the environment.

We were being threatened not at the national but at the global level, as one people on one planet, and we had to react at that level or perish. It primed my work to get support for the creation of the World Energy Network and the constitutional, global civilization.

As a result, in handling the hunger problem primarily by eliminating things like animal foods, we also went a long way in solving the destruction of the environment. Many of the greenhouse gases were also coming from the animals like I said. Across the board, the environment began a tremendous recovery as the use of animal foods receded into the past. This prehistoric idea of nutrition had just outlived its usefulness.

When I was touring and giving presentations, I would ask the audiences, by a show of hands:

"How many of you live in a cave?"
No hands went up.
"How many of you wear only animal skins as clothing?"
No hands went up.
"How many of you walk as your only form of travel?"
No hands went up.
"How many of you use tools made only from rock or bone?"
No hands went up.

I would respond by saying:
"If you have moved beyond the Stone Age level of thinking regarding habitation, clothing, transportation, and technology, why do you still cling to the Stone Age level of thinking regarding nutrition that is starving babies to death."

Interviewer:

"And the World Energy Network? It sounds like it was not all that necessary in solving the problems of animal based foods. It sounds like animal foods were equally important."

The Erastist:

"In a way, that is true. I was as strong on the subject of animal foods as anything else. It was something everyone could do. Everyone chooses the foods they eat. As people saw these old-fashioned foods also had effects on their bodies like they were having on the environment, they began to lose their attraction to them, especially when they learned eating animal foods ages your body. Our vegetable-based digestive system strains to process meat and that strain ages the body.

The World Energy Network was necessary to create a new system of providing power for the new future. I mentioned how it gave the impoverished people of the planet access to some labor-saving equipment and increased their food supply. It also led the way in eliminating fossil and nuclear fuels all over the world. These old-fashioned sources of power were like animal foods. They had come to the end of their usefulness and had instead become major, extinction level problems to handle.

Just as animal foods were one of the main causes of water pollution and ill health, the use of carbon-based fuels was the main cause of air pollution along with the methane I mentioned. The use of fossil-fuels and melting the Arctic methane around the planet dumped a non-stop flow of these greenhouse gases into the air. Remember, the idea then was you can throw something away, not as we now know, alà Einstein, that everything has to go somewhere and is part of the total system, the Universe. We had come to the point of having to change what we were discharging into the environment or die.

I saw a show on television about the use of hydrogen as a fuel. It said that when the automobile was first developed, there were experiments done on several possible fuels. Gasoline at that time was a waste product of refining oil. It seems hydrogen was discarded after the Hindenburg dirigible blew up. Then came electric cars. But the technology at that time was not equal to the task of providing adequate power to make electricity a major source of energy for automobiles. However, the Network's ability to generate enormous amounts electricity made them very practical.

They were equally efficient as any other car and were very quiet. I have many memories of hearing loud fossil fueled cars, trucks and motorcycles and their roaring engines with blue clouds of exhaust. It seemed to me that they considered the speed limit signs to be the minimum speed to do! But with the World Energy Network, in no time, the vehicles of the planet were humming along on a fuel that did not foul the air, change the water of the planet into acid, or make the climate heat up.

When the World Energy Network was completed, the solar, wind, tidal, hydroelectric, and geothermal sources of energy were tied into one continuous system of power production. That meant all the old systems of production based on fossil and nuclear sources were no longer needed. They had become obsolete along with nearly everything else. Remember, Fuller's research showed the incoming energy from the sun dwarfed the amounts of it stored in the fossil remains of dinosaurs or in the few tons of uranium on the planet."

Interviewer:

"It is wonderful to have access to unlimited, clean power. Once the World Energy Network was all connected, what did you see as the first task in capturing all of this incoming power of the Universe?"

The Erastist:

"I once heard this quote, "progress is preservation of order in change, and the preservation of change in order."

The World Energy Network was the crystal example of how to do that. First, we followed Fuller's idea of lining the seacoasts of the planet with small tidal generators that bobbed on the waves generating small amounts of electricity.

These tidal generators were themselves connected to larger, land-based generators creating massive amounts of electricity to be distributed to the planet. Fuller said this system alone would produce enough energy to replace fossil and nuclear fuels. Then there before us lay solar, wind, and geothermal energy sources.

The next, obvious step was the massive employment of solar technology. I saw a children's science show on public TV that said if you drew a circle a little bit bigger than 25 centimeters in diameter, it had about 100 watts of solar power in it. Now you think about the whole side of the Earth facing the sun and there is an outrageous amount of solar energy to be had.

One side of the Earth is always facing the sun. That meant there was a non-stop supply of free power to begin the cleaning up of the past. Fuller calculated that the Earth received two and one-half times the amount of energy that we were using then.

There were large territories of uninhabited desert land that were ready to have solar panels installed and connected into the World Energy Network. This power then was used to make more power. The old fossil driven power plants were refitted to be run by electricity. The desert solar panels fed power continually and the power plants ran continually. The World Energy Network simply sent out the power as it was needed.

The Sahara Desert, the Gobi Desert, the deserts in the Southwest of the United States, in the Middle East, in the Outback of Australia, and all the other desert areas on the planet were now not wasteland but part of the new energy lifeblood of our new future. And the technology did not disturb the environment at all.

The wind blew everywhere. There had already been quite a development in harnessing the wind before the global response got off the ground. Along with the solar arrays, wind turbines were included in the construction. We got twice the energy on the same pieces of land.

Next we added the hydroelectric power of the waterfalls of the world, the tidal power like in the Bay of Fundy, and the geothermal power of the Pacific Rim's Ring of Fire. All of this to run generators for the benefit of everyone on the planet.

I knew it was the end of the past and the beginning of the future promised by Einstein and Fuller. It meant electrifying the planet. It meant the creation of the Green Industrial Revolution. This was the name given to the explosive developments created by Fuller's, non-polluting technology that was able to transform reality from the obsolete one we were living in to the one we inhabit now."

Interviewer:

"How did electrifying the planet have such a quick effect on the really down and out?"

The Erastist:

"They had the power now to do things they had never been able to do before. For example, they were able to run pumps to provide clean water. That alone improved the quality of health of everyone. It also freed the women from having to walk many kilometers to get their water and carry it back many kilometers to their village. Now all they had to do was turn on the tap.

They also had pumps to irrigate their fields. I saw a show where two Asian farmers were irrigating their rice field by dipping a bag into a water supply on the other side of a small dike that they were standing on and then pulling it over by ropes they were holding to spill the water into the field to irrigate their crops.

Over and over, they pulled and dumped, pulled and dumped, pulled and dumped. Their whole day was about dipping, pulling, and dumping to irrigate their field. With their new electric water pump, provided by the new world government, they were able to irrigate more land and increase their status. Ask them what difference the World Energy Network's electricity made!

The Network and generators meant the end of human and animal power for the really down and out just like the technology did for the people after the beginning of the Industrial Revolution. As the Network was able to provide more and more power, more and more simple labor-saving devices relieved more and more people from drudgery. Now it has relieved us all over the planet from any drudgery."

Interviewer:

"What about the fossil and nuclear industries? Didn't they have some objections to all this talk about ending the use of fuels that provided their livelihood?"

The Erastist:

"For sure at first, they were expectantly very opposed. I guess the blacksmiths were not all that thrilled to see Henry Ford and all the other developers of the automobile putt-putting around.

But the time had come to end the use of fossil and nuclear fuels one way or another. Either we were going to eliminate them, or they were going to eliminate us. They had outlived their usefulness and had become the major threat to life on Earth including all of humanity which also included the executives of the energy companies.

Many of the executives of these industries also knew the handwriting was on the wall. Several had already made the moves to transform their companies into power companies for the future. They had the resources, and we had the need for their leadership.

They embodied the spirit of Bucky Fuller in all of this. Bucky said the goal was the improvement of the life of everyone to the disadvantage of no one. The transformation of the planet had to be a win-win situation for everyone, or it did not stand much of a chance of success. As these old industries were transformed, we had the time to anticipate the end of fossil and nuclear fuels and to plan for the transformation to something that served the needs of everyone, like the World Energy Network and the constitutional, global civilization.

Many industries had the time to transform their businesses into producing something that was needed for the general transformation of the planet. There was so much that needed attention that there was no lack of something to produce. Just as the new businesses of the Industrial Revolution grew out of the needs of the time, the environmental industries seemed to spring out of the ground. In the same way that armament industries rose to the challenge of defeating the Axis powers in World War II.

Some companies were affected very little. Power companies actually had their job simplified. With the World Energy Network supplying all the power, they only had to become distribution centers. Like the water companies, they did not have to make their product but only provide for its delivery. Instead of being climate change makers, they were now humming on clean power from the bountiful Universe flowing through the World Energy Network. They now were climate change curers.

This is not to say that it was all done without a lot of emotion and feeling. I have been shot at more than a few times in the process too. Old ways can die hard sometimes. But the positive results of the World Energy Network were so immediate that there was not much room for objection. And ideas like cyborg assistants caught the imaginations of the people who were being most affected by the transformation."

Interviewer:

"Cyborg assistants! What a great term. How did you get onto the idea of having all the work being done by machines and the humans get the paychecks?"

The Erastist:

"The same place I got most of my ideas, Bucky Fuller! Even as long ago as back then, Fuller said that 70% of what was then called work could be done by machines. The fact that the machines could do the work was not the real problem. The main concern was the so-called unemployment it would create. That was what most people feared.

It was much like when the owners of the early companies of the 19th Century had all the power and rights. The workers had none. The struggle to unionize was one of fortitude, violence and sacrifice. But their suffering did not go in vain either for their immediate goals or for the futuristic goals for which they were striving.

The biggest issue, the biggest obstacle, was the ownership of the profits. Under the pressure of the necessity to solve the problem, it was decided that if people were to lose their jobs because a machine could do it better and faster, then the machine did the work, and the unemployed worker would get the paycheck. This allowed the workers the freedom to pursue something that satisfied them and even made them consumers of the products the machines were producing.

We had enslaved animals and other humans for thousands of years for all kinds of reasons: war, economics, race, religion or sex. Now it was possible to have the machines do the labor and we get the goodies. And machines did not get tired or complain about their jobs either. Plus, the owners would still get their normal profits.

Fuller had observed that there was now a distinction that could be made between what we call work and what we call labor. They said that work is what you want to do with your time like artistic expression, sports, travel or whatever, and labor is what you have to do with your time to survive.

With systems like cyborg slavery providing the income, people were free to pursue their work, pursue their creative dreams. Today, the idea of having to do anything other than one's heart's desire is really foreign. It is as if childhood never has to end. I am ever amazed at how fast it all happened once the ball really got rolling."

Here's another song I do that explores this idea":

Plantation Life

I

Is there an artist inside of you?
Can you paint me your own picture?
Play me your own tune?
Oh, write me a story
Dance with me all night
And I promise I will make love with you
In a warm symphony of soft candlelight

Chorus:

No, I got to work at the factory
Got to put time on the machine
Must attend those staff meetings
Got to prove I'm one of the team
Later on when we retire
We'll catch up to all our dreams

II

Tell me where would you like to go to
Can you name me some new names?
Where would the wind blow you?
Oh, show me the highway
Dance with me again
And I promise I will go 'way with you
We'll be off together laughing hand in hand

III

Is there an artist inside of you?
Can you paint me your own picture?
Play me your own tune?
Oh, show me the highway

Dance with me all night
And I promise I will make love with you
We'll be off together on a rainbow flight

Chorus

Coda:

Is there an artist inside of you?

Interviewer:

"Wow! That just about says it all! With that, there's not much else left to say! Thank you for sharing your artistry.

Goodnight, everyone! We'll be back next week with more from the Erastist! We'll see you then! Goodnight!"

EPISODE FOUR THE MUSIC

Interviewer:

"I can see now how your thinking in those days was starting to be turned away from the old ideas we all were indoctrinated into as children by the cultures we happened to be born into. I really did like the lyrics to the song Plantation Life you ended our last episode with.

I'd like to hear some more about the birth of your professional music. It has been an integral part of your work and in capturing the minds and hearts of the people on the planet.

You talked about getting a guitar a year or so after hearing songs being played while you were in graduate school. How did the rest happen?"

The Erastist:

"Oddly enough that first guitar was, by the way, loaned to me by my music mentor and future partner, Dave. It was the same guitar they had started on and the one that was given to them by their father. As I have said, coincidence is God's way of remaining anonymous!

Dave and I formed a true brother relationship. We often said we were brothers from different mothers. We would meet once a week faithfully in Dave's second floor music room and were, as I thought, like kids in a tree house letting their imaginations run wild and that would then become songs. Dave and I wrote about a 100 songs together. Mostly, I wrote the lyrics and Dave created the music, sang the lyrics and engineered the recording of the songs.

The summer following my first divorce, I went with Lee's brother, Thomas, on a trip to Florida. The original idea was to sign onto shrimp boats and begin a life of adventure. On the way, however, we picked up a hitchhiker who steered us toward a different beach on the promise there would be ample opportunities to have sex and fun. Who were we to say no! And it was there on that beach that the life-shaping moment you asked about happened. The hitchhiker said we should go to Cocoa Beach.

82

We did. I was standing on the beach throwing Frisbee with Thomas. They were standing at the water's edge with their back to the ocean. They threw me the Frisbee and it arced way off to the right. I went over to get it and turned around.

Then I saw, in denim cutoffs, the prettiest pair of legs I had ever seen, with waist long, auburn hair, strolling by in the surf behind Thomas. I stood like a statue and stared as this beauty strolled through the surf and the sand. The sunlight sparkled around them like fireflies in the air. That is how I described it in the song I wrote later called Angel Hair.

Thomas started wondering why I wasn't throwing the Frisbee and what I was looking at. So, they turned around and saw the lady too. When Thomas turned back around, I was standing in front of them, handing them the Frisbee, and said, "I'm going for a walk."

The lady turned out to be Marie, the person who became my music muse and got me into songwriting. I have always called Marie the mother of my music. They were a singer-songwriter from the Nashville area who was in town only until the next morning. They were in town with their mother performing somewhere. Marie's mother, Joan, was a gifted musician, a recorded songwriter and played about six instruments at a professional level.

Marie's mom wrote "Heartbreak Hotel" made famous by Elvis Presley that made Presley famous too. And on that first record, Presley was on the A side of the record and Marie's mom was on the B-side. Marie's father was a highly recognized, master harmonica player. They played guitar too, but they were very well-established on the Nashville music scene as a harmonica virtuoso. Marie's parents played regularly on the Grand Ol' Opry radio show in Nashville. And Marie even got on the show at the age of four and sang.

During our next few hours together, Marie and I quickly made a definite connection. After our meeting, we, with Thomas, went back to where they were staying and they got out their guitar. Sitting outside by a walkway, Marie sang us some of their songs, which was the first time I had heard anyone perform a song they had written. Marie was very good on the guitar and their voice was superb. I told them I played some, but I mostly did some Kris Kristofferson songs.

Marie casually said they used to date Kris. They went on about Kris and about the other very well-known music friends they had in Nashville, whom I had only known from recordings. It seems that Kristofferson even had produced and recorded Marie performing her music.

So instead of sailing away to sea, I returned home with Marie's name and phone number. I stopped off and visited them on the way back to town and began a whole new life. Before this trip, Dave had asked me if I would be interested in doing some songwriting. They had read a poem I had written. This invitation, coupled with the dreams fostered by Marie, made for a life-changing moment that would create developments I hadn't even dreamed of at the time. One would be me sitting here now and talking about all of this to a global audience!

As soon as I got back to town, I called Dave and said I would <u>love</u> to get together and write some songs. We met in Dave's second floor music room and began banging on our guitars and scribbling down some lyrics. Like I said, Dave handled the music and I handled the lyrics. As someone once said, great things have simple beginnings.

We saw right away that we had the core of something good, but we also saw that we needed people who could really sing; we needed a group. We thought instead of reproducing another band with the standard make-up of drums and guitars, we would focus on a different approach. We would just use Dave and me on guitars, have the lead singers, and probably add a bass player and some simple percussion by the lead singers.

As it turned out, Dave had played music for a good while with a married couple who had some really good voices. They were, of course, Harold and Margie. It was at a party at their house where I spoke with Dave about getting together when I got back from Florida. Dave also suggested that we might add a bass player to provide a bottom to the music. But the core sound would be my rhythm guitar, a bass guitar, Dave's leads on a variety of instruments, and our collective vocals plus some simple percussion like tambourine and maracas.

The core of the sound was always Dave's music. They are one of those musicians who can play anything that has strings on it. Harold and Margie turned out to be very good tambourine and maracas players too. We knew it was only a matter of practice on our part. We knew we had a distinctive sound and equal to anything on the market.

So, Dave and Wylie, Dave's friend who came on board to play bass, keyboards and also sing, were in charge of the instrumental music. They made a first class musician out of me. The vocal arrangements were the bailiwick of Harold and Margie.

Harold had a two and a half octave range and an incredibly powerful voice. Once, when we were playing at one of those bars in the early days, Harold performed a complete set with their mic turned off and no one even knew it.

I always said that if Harold had been around at the same time as Elvis, you would have never heard of Elvis. And Margie had a voice that was so powerful and clear that they could have easily been an operatic diva.

I brought the vision and the original songs to the group and also served as the manager. But after Dave and I began writing, the creative juices of Harold and Margie also began to blossom. With Harold's perspectives and the feminine input of Margie, we had a wide and diverse pool of ideas to draw from. Added to the varied musical styles provided by Dave and Wylie, our repertoire list went through the roof. The only thing remaining was rehearsals and getting discovered."

Interviewer:

"So now you have put together a group. How did you get started right at first? And why did you call yourselves "The Shoes"? Everyone knows after you left the group, you became the biggest thing in contemporary music and a major factor in moving the planet to the constitutional, global civilization, but how did it all really happen?"

The Erastist:

"Yes, we did call ourselves "The Shoes". When the Beatles were starting to become The Beatles, Paul McCartney was asked why did they call themselves "The Beatles". McCartney answered that it didn't make any difference what name they chose. They were still the same band and the same sound. They said that the band could have called themselves "The Shoes" if they wanted to. That's the spirit we felt too when we named our group.

After I had met Marie and had the fire of music and songwriting lit, I never was the same. As you'll see, there have been a succession of marvelous women who have helped form me and my life. It goes back to those graduate school days. Lee was the first to encourage me to get a guitar and learn to play. And, including Lee, there have been a number of life-shaping moments that have come in the form of very loving women.

Right after Lee and I broke up, I got to know Regen. They taught at the same high school where I was teaching. We went out on a date that lasted for eight years. They taught me the ways of the world and opened my eyes to a lifestyle that has served me well ever since.

You see, Regen was not into monogamy either. They showed me that I can love and be loved on a general basis, like the whole human family of this planet, and be sexually intimate with some of them.

The biblical prophets had several sexual relationships, multiple wives and so on. I don't think the prophets had the corner on the ability to do that. Regen showed me through their love for me and their example that it can be done.

During one of those years that we were together, Regen even lived with another guy, and I never even knew it. Regen broke up with the guy because they wanted Regen to dump me. They said that they never put any restrictions on anyone else because they did not want anyone putting restrictions on them. Sounds like freedom to me!

Regen supported me in going for it with my music. I quit my teaching job to concentrate fully on the group and the music. Regen not only supported me in going for it, but they also even helped to support me with living space and feeding me for a long time. They let me have use of a spare bedroom in their apartment to store some of my clothes and to practice. Since we were fiery lovers too, staying with Regen was a very natural, marriage-level relationship.

We still saw other people and once Regen even put some clean sheets on their bed for me to spend the night with another lady I was seeing. Then, they went off to spend the night with another friend of theirs. As all of the theologies say, we are here to love one another, and I have experienced the reality of doing just that on an intimate basis with a number of wonderful human beings. Love is love, and fornication is fornication. Sin lies in the heart and not in the deed.

About a year after Regen and I began our relationship, I met Sunlight again. I had met them before during graduate school on one of those trips to visit Lee's brother, Thomas. Sunlight lived in an apartment in the same house as Thomas. But I was still married to Lee, and nothing developed between us....then.

I used to live on a street that had a huge art fair every fall. Several thousand people and many artists from all over the country come to attend and peddle their art. I used to say that I could stand outside my apartment building during the art fair and everyone I knew in town would walk by. My apartment building stood across from a fountain. While I was standing in front of my apartment building, I saw Sunlight standing at the fountain, and they saw me.

This time, however, we were both unattached and that afternoon we became attached. We saw one another for the next five years, and of course, remained in relationship off and on. During this time, I basically lived partly with Regen and partly with Sunlight.

It was after the divorce of my second, and last, marriage that Sunlight and I reconnected. I was with them when their stroke hit. I thought they were tipsy or had been smoking reefer, but when their arm knotted up tightly to one side, I knew Sunlight was having a stroke.

I called an ambulance immediately. The stroke paralyzed Sunlight's right side and slurred their speech, but Sunlight's brain remained almost as clear as ever. Eventually, I helped them move to live with a sister in a neighboring state.

Unfortunately, Sunlight passed away shortly after that. Broke my heart. But they were free from their pain and suffering.

All during this, the band was rehearsing for we knew that, even given the talent we had, we needed to present a superior product. One of the things I brought to the party was discipline. For decades, I had been carrying on a program of free weight training and was a competitive bodybuilder. It was clear to me that we needed to be very on purpose if we were going to make it in the music business.

One day, when Dave and I were over at Sunlight's, we got to talking about how much of a drag that disciplined part of my personality could be at times. They had even given the personality a name, "Schickelgruber". But then Sunlight said they wondered what it would be like if Schickelgruber would direct their energies toward solving the world's problems.

Right then, something in my brain clicked. Talk about a life-shaping moment!

Everything seemed to gel at that moment. All the information I had gotten in school and the study of Einstein and Fuller, all the power of music, books, and video to shape and influence the thinking of people. It was another spiritual experience like at that moment at the high school retreat I mentioned.

From then on, I knew that my life, art, and energies would be shaped and directed toward moving this planet to a new reality of peace and prosperity, with the creation of the World Energy Network and the constitutional, global civilization."

Interviewer:

"It's funny how seemingly separate events can become really parts of one story. What did Fuller call it?"

The Erastist:

"Synergetics- individual things in a single, unified system."

Interviewer:

"At that point, you had a group and a focus. What was the first thing you did to get started?"

The Erastist:

"Being the manager too, I would also be the one who handled the bookings for the group, and I went out to the bars to do just that. Since the other members of the group had played almost entirely at parties, I thought the bars were a natural place to start. There was a small beer bar on a strip where many of the bands in town played. I went out and talked to the owner of the Down to Earth Pub about us performing there. Don't you think it's really ironic that we started in a place called that? Like the person said, coincidence is God's way of remaining anonymous.

The parties, where Dave, Harold, and Margie had played for years, had a number of family and friends who were very willing to come out and hear us. We drank the pub dry, and the owners said they couldn't handle the size of the crowd. That began a series of similar experiences where we stood all the bars on that strip on their heads.

Then, we started to expand to other areas and venues. We had a chance to play some college dates and then got into one of the big-time bars downtown. The results were all the same. Hot shows with very ecstatic audiences. There was one place in particular that became our home port and from which I would spring onto the national stage and, of course, from there to the planet.

What fun days those were. I was physically young, single, and the leader of the hottest band in town! Those shows were some of the best times I ever had. I know I eventually played every big show there is and then some, but those shows were so innocent and charged with the raw power of the newness of it all.

There was a pack of soldiers who came in from the local army base every weekend to go crazy with the music. One guy even took his last leave before shipping out overseas to come hear us. I still remember him dancing on the table.

During all of this, I had also still been dating Marie in Tennessee. They came up to town occasionally and certainly got more than their chance to hear us perform. Marie, in time, drifted away from trying to make it in music and wound up marrying a guy and moving to Florida. But before that, they introduced me to a friend, Johnnie, in Nashville, who worked in the music business. We became good friends too but not lovers.

After Marie had moved to Florida, I continued to go to Nashville to see what I could do to get the band farther down the road. I called Johnnie one day and said I was headed to town the coming weekend and if they were free, I thought we might get together.

They said they'd love to but couldn't because they were going to be tied up in the studio all weekend recording a nationally known country music star. However, they said Marie had told them about my group and added that if I brought them a tape, they would pass it around town and see what could be done with it.

Well, I knew that was an offer that could not be refused! But the group did refuse the offer. They said they didn't think Johnnie could deliver on what they said. I think it was really a fear of success. Very often, someone strives to reach a level of success only to be afraid of it when it arrives.

I said they were not serious about making it in the music business and left the group shortly afterwards. After that, outside of a few road trips, they continued playing at the local level for several years.

Not too long after leaving the group, I remarried for the second time. In the transformational seminar work I did, I met Donna. We eventually paired off, I moved in with them, and we got married. I thought I had found the other half of my sky, as a Chinese poet once put it.

Then came the surprise that Donna could sing! We began working on my music and they were instrumental in getting us bookings. We went to Russia together and then toured in Florida with our newly made Russian musician friends. But after that trip, Donna then told me they were not doing music with me any longer. That began our decline into divorce.

It was about this time I started performing solo in senior retirement homes. Every place had an activities director whose job was to book people like me to entertain the residents. Willie Nelson said that if people are not familiar with your music, you need to do music they are familiar with. That was exactly what I did. I did music they all knew and could sing along with.

The shows reminded me of people sitting around a campfire singing songs. Some residents were close to being unconscious, but when the music started, their foot would start tapping or their hand began patting their leg. Some even woke up to really being there and some even tried singing along. I eventually learned this was an actual therapy for their mental wellness. It transformed my relationship to what I was doing in my performances and my world peace work.

I soon linked up with Wayne, the bass player I had met when Dave and I visited Dave's friend, Edward, one night. Wayne said they had heard of our group, The Shoes, and we hit it off well. Shortly after that meeting, Dave's friend, Edward, died. After that and me leaving the group, Wayne and I reconnected.

I told them about Johnnie's offer and would they be interested in helping record a tape to give to Johnnie. Wayne was interested! and so was Everett, a very good drummer friend of Wayne's. We began working and soon had a good representative tape to present. Here are some samples of the songs I sent.

The first ones were commercially sufficient. A record producer in Nashville told me once that the main purpose of the songwriter was to find out different ways of saying "I love you". Here are the songs on that theme I sent.

The first, as I said, is a song I wrote for Marie, my lovely music muse. Again, it is called "Angel Hair":

<u>Angel Hair</u>

I

It was by the sea I saw her
Strolling thru the surf and the sand
With the sunlight sparkling
Like fireflies in the air
It was all I could do
Stand and stare
At the lovely lady
With the angel hair
Chorus: And she sang me her songs
Filled me with her dream
Showed me a life
Only writers of songs can see
I was lost upon a sea of doubt
Oft times drowned in despair
Well, this is my song to you
My lovely angel hair

II

We spent that summer together
Strolling thru love hand in hand
Her songs pouring in me
Like rainbows I swear
An' the colors grew 'n' grew
Giving dreams to dare
Dreams like those of
My lovely angel hair
Chorus:

92

The next song was one I had written for my dear soul mate, Sunlight. I think I wrote this, "Storms of Time", after she had passed away. We both shared an affection for the moon:

Storms of Time

I

On starlit nights
When the moon is bright
My thoughts drift away to you
And through the night
If the spirit's right
We once again are tw
Chorus:
Oh, storms of time, drift away
Leave me now, leave me today
Storms of time, drift to sea
Leave her, the moon, and me

II

The moon's sweet light
Softens the night
And shadows fill the air
And through the sky
Our spirits fly
And once again we're there
Chorus:
Oh, storms of time, drift away
Leave me now, leave me today
Storms of time, drift to sea
Leave her, the moon, and me

Coda:

On starlit nights
When the moon is bright
My thoughts drift away
To you

I once had someone say to me that I was their slice of heaven. Isn't that one of the sweetest things anyone can say to anyone else? Here's the song that grew out of that acknowledgement, "My Slice of Heaven":

<u>My Slice of Heaven</u>

I

You are my lover
The light in my life
You brighten my days
Light up my nights
You are the reason
I do what I do
The light of my life
Is you

II

You are my lover
The warmth of my heart
You ignite my passion
Heat up my dark
You are the reason
I do what I do
The warmth of my heart
Is you

Chorus:

You are my slice of Heaven
The other half of my sky
Soul mate, True love
I will love you
Beyond the day that I die

III

You are my lover
The life in my eyes
The beauty of the oceans
The blue of the skies
You are the reason
I do what I do
The life in my eyes
Is you

Then I added two erastistic songs. The first was a song dealing with the reality paradigm shift coming from the works of Einstein and Fuller. Time to put aside the old ideas we were brainwashed in regardless of our "country" or culture. It is called "Color Outside the Lines":

Color Outside The Lines

I

There comes times in history
To leave the past behind
Retire old ways of thinking
Open new doors in our minds
Time for new answers
An' color outside the lines

Chorus:

Reality
Handed down to you and me
But now we can have
Anything we can dream
Build anything
To our design
Look like it's time
To color outside the lines

II

There comes times in our lives
To make up our minds
That this ain't working out
And things are not fine
Time for new answers
An' color outside the lines

After Johnnie took the tape to several producers, one, Rob Wren, liked what they heard. At that point, I did not have any idea the impact I would have on the world, but I sure did. In a matter of no time, it seems, I had hit music and road trips. Rob introduced me to an agent, Brian Glockenspiel, to handle my road-trip bookings.

Brian, with the audiences guaranteed by the success of the music, had little trouble getting me booked as an opening act for many of the musicians I had listened to on the stereo and radio and most had autographed my guitar. You probably know I have people who have influenced me to autograph my guitar.

Since I was becoming better known around the nation, I was also becoming something of a hometown hero. A local organization, that raised money for food to give to people who needed it, held a benefit concert once a year. They had gotten globally known Harry Chapin to come and perform. This show afforded me the opportunity to get my first autograph of an established artist.

Actually, the first person to sign their name was Dave, from The Shoes, who signed it right up at the top of the guitar. I asked why they signed it there. Dave said when I did get on television, people would see their name! Then came my kids, Lewis and Ann, their mom, Lee, then Marie, Regen, Sunlight, Harold, Margie, Wylie, my parents, siblings and many others.

Harry said that they would rather try something and fail than look back ten years later and say they wished they had tried. That hit me square in the heart. And Harry's music making a difference in dealing with hunger was also reason enough to have their name on my guitar.

Harry founded World Hunger Year and got hunger right out in the front of the old United Nations. Harry said that if those at the top of the entertainment society are not responsible to the needs of those who put them there, then they do not need to be supported by them. Harry would do every third concert as a benefit.

So, this show in my hometown for feeding people was a natural for Harry and a good break for me. I opened the concert and the audience loved it. Harry was also impressed and asked me to open for them for the rest of their tour. I did and had a marvelous time. Even sold some albums.

The next few years were taken up in recording and concert tours. My music and musicianship got better and better. I collected the autographs on my guitar, and sometimes the friendships, of a number of leading artists.

The alphabetical tour of Sunshine, my guitar, in alphabetical order, is Muhammed Ali, Harry Chapin, George Carlin, Lana Chapel, John Denver, Bob Dylan, Steve Earle, Misha Feigin, Buckminster Fuller, Larry Gatlin, Arlo Guthrie, Richie Havens, Kris Kristofferson, Don McLean, Willie Nelson, Peter, Paul, and Mary, John Prine, Pete Seegar, Carl Sagan, Stephen Stills, James Taylor, and Mason Williams. One person I failed to get was Chuck Berry, the true father of rock'n'roll and, I think, rap. And I never got Paul Simon's name either.

Today there is no more room for names. After I got Richie Havens' name on my guitar, I started doing some heavy strumming like Richie did. I managed to scrape off a couple of names including Marie's! Whenever I see them again, I am going to loosen the strings so then they can re-sign their name. Then, I will retighten the strings after they sign it again behind the sound hole. Marie's name will be protected from any further harm!

As you probably noticed, I also got the names of non-musicians too. First, I got the name of Buckminster Fuller himself. We had a thirty-five-minute conversation where I felt like a kindergarten kid talking to the dean of the university. Sunlight and I were on our way to San Francisco for a traveling vacation and for them to relocate there. We then went to Philadelphia for me to meet Bucky, which gave me a chance to see my kids in Wisconsin too.

Bucky talked with me for a while and then I asked them to sign the guitar. They autographed it, and then scratched a square with lines going from corner to corner. Then Bucky looked up at me with those Mount Palomar eyeglasses, an ear-to-ear grin, and said "Tetrahedron"! This is the basic geometric structure of Bucky's architecture.

Meeting Muhammed Ali was fun. I stopped by a former mayor's house in my hometown, who happened to live in my neighborhood and who was a friend of Muhammed. Muhammed was in town for some reason, and, after introducing the mayor to my world peace efforts, I asked them for a way to meet Ali. They wrote out a note to Ali's travelling companion, Harold Bermingham. As it turned out actually, at that moment the mayor was writing the note, Muhammed and Harold were flying out of the city to Chicago. But the letter served me later when I went to Chicago to see if I could connect with Muhammed.

Muhammed was in Chicago to be the Grand Marshall for the World Patriotism Parade. I entered the school where an organizational meeting for the parade was being held. The place was abuzz with the fact that Muhammed was actually there. I asked the person at the registration desk if Harold Bermingham was there, and this guy behind me says "I'm Harold". The coincidence of that stunned me. I showed them the letter from the ex-mayor, and they told me when and where to show up to meet Muhammed.

Howard told me to come back to the hotel at 8:00 the next morning. They gave me their room number too. I showed up right on time with my guitar. I knocked on the door and there stood Harold. They pointed down to the end of the hallway and said Muhammed's room was the last room on the right. They said to tell Muhammed that Harold had sent me and that we could talk.

In those days, I was in the midst of being a hippie. I had shoulder length hair, a full beard, gold-rimmed, circular eyeglasses, all denim clothes and tennis shoes. I knocked on the door, and there stood Muhammed. They were combing their still wet hair from having just gotten out of the shower.

I introduced myself and said Harold thought we could talk. Muhammed invited me in.

I think I have mentioned my days of competitive bodybuilding. I was struck by how huge of a person Muhammed was! I felt again like a small kid in the presence of a large adult. I told Ali of my work to create the constitutional, global civilization, and they said that the world needed more people like me. I then asked them to autograph my guitar. It was a simple, unelaborated signature. Muhammed was like that: real, down to Earth, and with a quick sense of humor.

100

I mentioned to Muhammed that I would also like to get Kris Kristofferson's autograph too. Muhammed immediately responded saying, "Let's call him!" and picked up the phone. I then said one of the most stupid things I have ever said. I told Muhammed it was 5:00 in the morning in Los Angeles. They agreed and then hung up the phone. I don't think Kristofferson would have minded having Muhammed Ali phoning them that early. Certainly blew that one!

Muhammed said they were going to Detroit the next day for the 50th anniversary of the founding of the Nation of Islam and asked me if I would like to come along and perform for the celebration. Who was I to say no?! Certainly, I accepted.

Ali then asked me, probably from my appearance, how I was doing with money. I told them I had a bus ticket to get back home and there was a little money there. Muhammed reached into their pocket and pulled out a wad of bills about eight centimeters in diameter. They peeled off a bill and handed me $100. They then said they didn't want to run too short and handed me another $100 bill!

Muhammed next asked if I had had breakfast. I told them I hadn't, and they invited me to go downstairs we would get some breakfast. They ordered, I think, steak and eggs. I told Muhammed I was surprised they were still eating meat. They said they had tried to stop but couldn't. Harold was in the booth with us too with a lady they had spent the night with. Muhammed introduced me as Kris Kristofferson. The lady said I looked different in the movies. I said the camera does that.

Then it was time to head to the limos. When we walked out of the hotel, Muhammed asked the door person working outside if there was a restroom on the first floor. They said there was. Muhammed said: "Don't leave without me." As if we would!

While we were waiting, a friend of mine came out of the hotel and was very surprised to see me. I was a bit surprised to see them too. They were living with a college friend of mine in Oregon at the time Sunshine and I went to California after meeting Buckminster Fuller in Philadelphia. They astonishingly me asked why I was there.

Before I could answer their question as to why I was there, someone started tapping me on the shoulder. I turned around and it was Muhammed asking me if I was coming. I told my friend I had no time to explain and had to go. I left them with a stunned look on their face and never saw them again.

Ali has been quoted a lot. One of his statements has echoed to me over the years. They said, "The person who has no imagination has no wings." Like Fuller and synergetics, Ali focused on the big picture. I saw the goal of my work was to feed the imaginations of the people of the planet with the vision of the World Energy Network and the creation of the constitutional, global civilization. The big picture!

I got to meet Carl Sagan when I was in Russia. I had gone there to perform for the World Population Conference. Sagan was one of the primary organizers and very accessible. We spoke for a while, had a few pictures taken, and that was that. The hubba-bubba of the conference took both of us into different directions. But Sagan did autograph my guitar."

Interviewer:

"I can't tell you how thankful we all are for your time and insight. You certainly have led a fantastic life!

This concludes this episode, my friends. Join us next week for more adventures in the fantastic life of The Erastist!

Goodnight!"

EPISODE FIVE
TheConstitution for theFederation of Earth

Interviewer:

"You often refer to constitutional, global civilization. Like many citizens, I haven't actually read the Earth Constitution myself.

Can you elaborate on it?"

The Erastist:

"Certainly! Creating the <u>constitutional</u>, global civilization, as you put it, was like inventing a new game and the Earth Constitution was the rule book. It was created through the efforts of Dr. Glen T. Martin of Radford University. The Earth Constitution begins with a preamble, a concise statement of the reasons for the Constitution. It is written in pretty formal English, so I'll give a lay person's interpretation.

The Constitution starts by saying that humanity was at a turning point in history, on the threshold of a new world order of peace, prosperity, justice and harmony. You can see why I was behind the Constitution! That was another way of saying having a world devoid of hunger, poverty, pollution and war.

The preamble goes on to talk about the interdependence of all the people on the planet and the abuse of science and technology in producing weapons of mass destruction and bringing humanity to the brink of ecological and social catastrophe. It says the concept of security through military defense is now, and for me always has been, an illusion. As one person said, "Either war is obsolete or we are."

Then, the Constitution speaks of the disparity between the rich and the poor. It speaks of our obligation to prosperity for all humanity. It states that there are no differences in humans, what I, Einstein and Fuller, call the creative, intelligent energy beings powering the body, and we now can have unity in diversity. As I always say, one people on one planet!

We can all look different and speak different languages, but we, as creative, intelligent energy beings, share the same basic human rights and identity without discrimination. And with the abundant resources now from

Einstein's science and the technology of Fuller, everyone can have access to wealth like we have access to air.

The preamble concludes by saying the greatest hope for survival of life on Earth is the establishment of a democratic world government. For me, of course, that is the same as the establishment of the constitutional, global civilization."

Interviewer:

"I can't help but saying it sounds like something you could have written. What is the rest of the document like?"

The Erastist:

"Next comes the body of the Constitution. It is divided into 19 particular Articles to outline aspects of the world government. Article 1 is the "Broad Functions of the Earth Federation", the name given for the planetary government of the constitutional, global civilization. The first and foremost function was the ending of war. Like national societies did when they created their "country", war on the planet is outlawed between the member "countries" of the Federation. And, in a brief time, all the "countries" were in the Federation.

Now this sanity of eliminating war was legally defined into the new global society. An attack by one "country" on another would be considered an attack on all of the Federation which would react as needed. From there began the disarmament of the world's militaries that began the shift from them being killingry organizations to livingry organizations as I have said. The Federation provides peaceful resolutions to disputes, resolutions like the World Energy Network. People soon learned the advantages of living as cooperative erastists far outweighed living as competitive patriots.

The Federation is to protect human rights like life, liberty, security, democracy and equal opportunity based on what you know and what you can do and not on your looks or where you come from. The Federation is to obtain equal economic and social development and diminish social

105

differences. I saw this as an endorsement for the World Energy Network too. And it was a goal that was achieved!

The Federation is also there to regulate world interactions such as trade, communications and other global processes. Of course, the Federation is there to protect the environment, to keep the Earth, and I quote, "a safe, healthy and happy home for humanity". Simply put, the Federation is there to devise and implement peaceful solutions to all global problems.

Article 2 is the "Basic Structure of the Earth Federation". First and right off the bat is the Federation will encompass the entire planet: people, oceans and land. Now we had a legal claim to being one people on one planet. It was no longer a matter of opinion but was now law.

The Constitution goes on to say the Federation will be a non-military and democratic entity with sovereignty, or ultimate political decision-making, residing in the people of the planet. It basically says the government exists to provide the highest level of security to each and every one of us.

The authority and powers of the government are limited to those defined in the Constitution. The national governments had to operate within the structure of the Earth Constitution with the Federation being there to make sure everything ran smoothly. Nationalism was elevated to planetism and patriotism to erasism.

Article 2 lists the basic, political structure of the World Federation. This includes the planet being constructed of World Electoral and Administrative Districts with elected officials in each one. The districts are then organized into Electoral Regions and then into Magna-Regions. The boundaries of the districts and regions would follow natural boundaries "as far as practicable". There are to be five Continental Divisions on the planet.

Article 3 is the "Organs of the Federation", just a list of the different bodies of the Federation. This will be covered in greater detail in some of the following Articles. Here is the list from Article 3:

1.   The World Parliament- In the final version of the
Constitution, the delegates would only debate the laws and then
submit them to the planetary population for a vote.
2.   The World Executive
3.   The World Administration
4.   The Integrative Complex
5.   The World Judiciary
6.   The Enforcement System
7.   The World Ombudmus

Article 4 is the "Grant of Specific Powers to the Earth Federation".
This is a detailed coverage of Article 1. The first specific power is to
prevent wars and armed conflicts among any groups. The Federation is to
supervise disarmament and prohibit possession of weapons of mass
destruction and regulate all lethal weapons decided upon by the World
Parliament and voted on by the people of the planet. This is mainly
decided based upon the massacres of innocent citizens, especially school
children, with military-style weapons you could buy in a store like a candy
bar.

The Federation is also to provide peaceful and just solutions of
disputes between any parts of the global society, as I have said. It is to
supervise boundary disputes and conduct plebiscites, or voting, by the area's
population, to decide where the boundary lines would be. And similarly,
peaceful solutions would be found for any problems that arose.
The Federation is to oversee the electoral process for the members
of government at all levels, particularly for each House of the World
Parliament. It is to codify world law to be approved by the vote of the
planet's population. Again, the World Parliament members formulate the
world laws but only have their individual votes like anyone else on the
planet in making the final, legal decision."

Interviewer:

"This is all pretty standard reality now. It's hard to believe that once we were so backward. So, please continue."

The Erastist:

"Article 4 continues by saying the Earth Federation would provide assistance in the event of large scale calamities like famine, drought or other natural disasters. It is to guarantee and enforce civil liberties and the basic human rights defined in the Constitution in Article 12, "The Bill of Rights for the Citizens of the Earth". I'll talk more about them when we reach Article 12.
The Federation also is to promote global improvement in working conditions, nutrition, education, economic security and other conditions defined in Article 13, "The Directive Principles for the Earth Federation". Again, I'll talk more about all that when we get there too.

It is also the duty of the Federation to regulate and supervise global transportation, communications, postal services and migrations of people. The migrations soon disappeared after the planet had created the World Energy Network and a constitutional, global civilization. With a society founded on the resources of the Universe and recycling, the standard of living became the same for everyone all around the world.

Now there were no migrations from one part of the planet to another caused by drought, other climatic changes, or political suppression, but because of the regulation and supervision of planetary economics and the security provided by the Earth Constitution, there was no longer a need to migrate to somewhere better. Things became fine where you were, at home.
The Federation also is to plan and regulate the natural resources of the planet and, by implication, the resources in the solar system. These resources are deemed as the common heritage

of all humanity. They are for the benefit of both the present and future generations. The Constitution created the World Economic Development Organization to serve equally all the people in the Federation, every last one of us on this planet.

Article 4 goes on to say the Federation would develop and implement solutions to the global food supply, population growth, water supplies, the conservation of the oceans and the atmosphere. After the construction of the World Energy Network and its abundant supply of clean, renewable energy, these concerns soon became extinct. The pollution stopped. By ending hunger, the population stabilized. Everyone had access to abundant, clean water. And the oceans and atmosphere were pure once more.

The Federation is also to conduct cosmic explorations that would produce an explosion of mineral resources to raise the standard of living for everyone. My original vision of a constitutional, global civilization devoid of hunger, poverty, pollution, and war was now becoming our legal reality!"

Interviewer:

"I really appreciate your coverage of the World Constitution. The reality it created is certainly far superior to the many forms of government that preceded it when the planet was artificially divided into a few hundred independent, sovereign countries. It really did make us legally one people on one planet.

Please, do go on and describe the other parts of this historically crucial document."

The Erastist:

"I totally agree. Ruling the planet by law is so much better than using the force of arms!

The next section of the Earth Constitution is Article 5, "The World Parliament". The Parliament is designed to prepare and enact detailed legislation in all areas granted to the Federation. Again, they are to prepare the legislation that is to be voted on by the people all around the world.

Once passed, the World Parliament is to fulfill the legislation's vision. It is also supposed to review national constitutions developed before the creation of the Federation to be sure they align with the Earth Constitution.

This process also applies to the different branches of the Federation and the approval of its budget. The World Parliament is also to create or abolish the various branches as may be needed for the best functioning of the Federation. In addition, it is to name the heads of all the branches except those that are chosen by elections. They can remove such department heads from office if need be.

The World Parliament is to be composed of three Houses: The House of the Peoples to represent the population of the Earth directly and equally, the House of Nations to represent the member "countries" that composed the Federation of the Earth, and the House of Counsellors to represent the highest good and best interests of humanity as a whole.

The Constitution then outlines the specifics of the Houses regarding members and the length of their service time. Voting is open to all people on the planet 18 and older.

Article 5 concludes with the procedures of the World Parliament which I need not detail here.

Article 6 describes the functions and powers of the "World Executive" branch as defined in the Earth Constitution and codified by the World Parliament. The executive branch is to put into action the legislation of the World Parliament and to propose new legislation to them. They are also to supervise all of the departments in the World Administration and to submit annually a comprehensive budget to the World Parliament. The department is to be held accountable to the World Parliament for its expenditures.

The World Executive is to consist of a Presidium of five members and an Executive Cabinet from twenty to thirty members from the World Parliament. Of the five members of the Presidium, one is to be designated as President and the remaining four to be Vice-Presidents. The Presidency would rotate every year with each Vice-President to serve in turn as President. Each of the five members would be from the five different Continental Divisions to provide global representation.

The decisions of the Presidium would be taken collectively based on the majority. Nominations for Presidium membership would be made by the House of Counsellers. The number of nominees would be two or three times the number to be elected. The three Houses of government would elect the Presidium's new members. Any member of the Presidium could be removed for a just cause. The term of the office would be for five years and limited to two consecutive terms.

In the Executive Cabinet, no more than two members, out of the twenty to thirty other members, could be from any single nation in the Federation. Each member would serve as the head of a department. Nominations for membership would be made by the Presidium with no more than two times the number to be elected. Elections would be a simple majority of the three Houses of the World Parliament. Any vacancies would be filled within sixty days.

The World Executive would not at any time violate any provision or world law of the World Parliament or the Earth Constitution. They would have no veto power over any legislation passed by the people and could not dissolve the World Parliament or any House of it. They could not act contrary to decisions made by the World Courts. I thought the Earth Constitution really reflects the lessons regarding checks and balances learned by the democracies from the World War II dictatorships before the establishment of the constitutional, global civilization."

Interviewer:

"I really enjoy hearing you do this. I think when all of this comes out in the forthcoming book, it will be a great resource and of historical importance.

Please do continue!"

The Erastist:

"Yes, I am enjoying it too. In the future, this can be a real resource.

So, next is Article 7, "The World Administration". It is to carry out the detailed goals of world legislation and world law. It would be under the direction of the World Executive, and it would be composed of all the departments needed to administer the work of the Federation. Every major agency is headed by a Minister, who is also a member of the Executive Cabinet or a Vice-President of the Presidium.

Here is a list of the departments of the World Administration:

1.   Disarmament & War Prevention- The transformation of the military from killingry to livingry!
2.   Population- They did a lot to end hunger, poverty and pollution on the planet.
3.   Food and Agriculture- They also did a lot to eliminate hunger.
4.   Water Supplies and Waterways- They cleaned up the planet's waters like the 8 billion tons of plastic that was dumped into the water each year out of the 48 billion tons that was dumped into the environment, among other things.
5.   Health and Nutrition-They eventually eliminated animal foods which was a big step in eliminating hunger and several environmental problems. In no time, the health of everyone, particularly the children, improved remarkably.

6.   <u>Education</u>- This is where a lot of my work was used. I have always been a teacher and I just merely declared the world my classroom. I got to spend some time making sure everyone on the planet had access to a quality education that suited their needs and was fun.

7.   <u>Cultural Diversity and the Arts</u>- A lot of my music and videos found a home here. As I am a human, I am by nature creative and I was so fortunate to have found music. Or, maybe I should say, music found me!

8.   <u>Habitat and Settlements</u>- Fuller's geodesic architecture provided decent homes and buildings for the whole planet. Everyone got a place to call their own home. And the World Energy Network gave them the comfort they deserved.

9.   <u>Environment and Ecology</u>- They helped to make the World Energy Network a reality. The environmental value of the Network was rapidly recognized for its power to save the ecological health of the planet. This meant it would save all the life, including human life, on this planet too.

10.   <u>World Resources</u>-These also included extra-planetary resources. Remember we inhabit a Universe made of the same stuff. Once the constitutional, global civilization was founded, we had the ability to harvest that wealth all around us and recycle it.

11.   <u>Oceans and Seabeds</u>- They cleaned up the oceans and made them healthy again. This meant the basis of our ecosystem was healthy. They worked in conjunction with the Water Supplies and Waterways Department in restoring the health of the world's waters.

12.   <u>Atmosphere and Space</u>- They helped to eliminate fossil and nuclear fuel use and started the harvesting of the local resources of mineral wealth, like the asteroids, the moon and the other planets.

13. <u>Energy</u>-They were also very instrumental in getting the World Energy Network completed. After its completion, it began supplying an abundance of clean power to the whole planet.

14. <u>Science and Technology</u>- Of course Einstein's science was the rule of the day and Fuller's technology the blueprint for an advanced, global civilization. Their work, as I have been saying, was the science and technology that made the World Energy Network and the constitutional, global civilization a reality.

15. Genetic Research & Engineering- This research was able to reveal basic truths in the human genome and was able to lay the foundation for our planetary society made up of genetically perfect human beings.

16. Labor and Income- We've already talked about Fuller's cyborg slavery, which I have renamed cyborg assistants. After it replaced human labor, and the humans still got their paychecks and eventually were made billionaires like everyone else, they were free to follow their creative internal reality and play from birth to death. We had achieved a reality where childhood never had to end. My song, Born to Play, is based on this new reality.

17. Economic & Social Development- They worked in conjunction with the Labor and Income Department and the Commerce and Industry Departments to put everyone on the planet on easy street as soon as possible. They were crucially instrumental in eliminating poverty all over the planet.

18. Commerce and Industry- I just covered their role in #17 too.

19. Transportation and Travel- As Fuller's technology produced more free time for everyone, they naturally wanted to see the world, their new home. And with the power provided by the World Energy Network, they had the means to do just that. Soon there was a steady flow of millions of people traveling to all parts of the world. It began the process by which becoming one people on one planet was now actual reality instead of idealistic theory.

20. Multi-National Corporations- The corporations were held to a higher moral method of doing business instead of the scarcity, competition-based systems of pre-Einsteinian and Fulleresque thinking. Operating on economic system based on cooperative abundance, they and their corporations prospered more than ever.

21. Communications and Information- With the arrival of the cell phone, as I may have mentioned, humans had for the first time a global means of personal communication. It was, as I will elaborate on later, a crucial component in creating the constitutional, global civilization. In almost no time, any one person could call any other one person on the planet.

Tthey both had open access to any information. It created a true democracy by providing voting on the legislation submitted by the World

Parliament to anyone on the planet who had a phone. In a very short time, that meant everyone on Earth.

22. Human Rights- The whole purpose of the World Constitution and the creation of the Federation was to secure rights at the human level. As creative, intelligent energy beings, we are all equal. Our rights are guaranteed at the level of being and not on the levels of biological identity, scarcity-based economics and obsolete social ideas of the past.

23. Distributive Justice- In securing our rights, it is imperative that the law be equally and fairly administered. The operative word is "justice". That is the guiding light of the whole legal system.

24. World Service Corps- This is an outgrowth of the old Peace Corps. And like the Peace Corps, the majority of members are young. The college students identified with erasism and were eager to create the constitutional, global civilization. It took very little effort to enlist millions of the young around the world to make the historical efforts needed to reach our goals.

25. World Territories, Capitals & Parks- These were the primary targets of many groups on the planet. They are united into this department and are able to increase their impact tremendously. A great deal of untouched wilderness was allowed to stay that way. The monuments in the capitals of the planet were like a huge museum, and, as fine artwork, preserved for future generations.

26. Exterior Relations- This department didn't last very long, because after the planet became ruled by the Federation, there were no longer any "exterior" relations until we might possibly encounter beings from other planets.

27. Democratic Procedures- As I said before, the communications revolution made a true democracy feasible and achievable. The processes laid out in the World Constitution are very clear about the democratic procedures to be employed. The people will do the voting and the computers in the office of the World Executive will tabulate the results.

28. Revenue- With the explosion of wealth from recycling and harvesting the minerals of the asteroids, moon, and other planets, this department managed the flow of wealth around the planet.

As you can see, several of the departments worked together to create a constitutional, global civilization devoid of hunger, poverty, pollution, and war."

Interviewer:

"I am really impressed at the magnitude of the Earth Constitution. I get the very real feeling in being in a time like the writing and acceptance of the national constitutions.

Well, I suppose we are at Article 8 now?"

The Erastist:

"And so we are.

Article 8 covers "The Integrative Complex". It is a grouping of the agencies essential for the functioning of the Federation. Each agency is to be headed by a Cabinet Member. The World Parliament may add further responsibilities to the Complex.

Here is a list of the various agencies of the Integrative Complex:

1.   The World Civil Service Administration-

It defines standards for the personnel of the World Government. It is headed by a ten member commission in addition to the Cabinet

Minister. The term of office for all the member commissions is five years and an option to serve consecutive terms.

2.   The World Boundaries and Elections Administration-

It defines the boundaries of the electoral regions. The boundaries are periodically adjusted every five or ten years. It also defines procedures for the nomination and election of members of the World Parliament to the Houses of Peoples and Counsellors.

Before each election, it prepares a pamphlet detailing the election. It is to define the rules for the world political parties and procedures for legislative initiatives by the Citizens of the Earth. It is to conduct plebiscites when requested, to settle boundary disputes, and conduct a global census every five years.

3.   Institute on Governmental Procedures on World Problems-

This agency is to conduct courses for all the personnel of the World Government to have a better understanding of the functions of government. It is to bring in qualified persons to conduct the courses. I was fortunate enough to be asked to conduct a course and to speak at a few of the other courses.

4.   The Agency for Research and Planning-

It will serve the Federation in any matter requiring research and planning for any other agency. It is to compile and maintain a comprehensive inventory of world resources, which later came to include extra-terrestrial resources as well, and they made long-range plans for sharing all of the resources for the benefit of all the people on the planet.

It is to prepare a list of world problems and propose solutions. It will prepare legislative measures for all of the departments of the Federation. I contributed a lot to this work as well.

5.   The Agency for Technological and Environmental Assessment-

This one is to maintain a registration of all significant technological innovations like the World Energy Network. It will assess the pros and cons of each innovation especially in regard to its impact on the environment and the human population. They are to prepare recommendations to the other agencies of the Federation for the use of any new technology that could be of benefit to them. It was a primary force in ending hunger, poverty, pollution and war.

6.   The World Financial Administration-

This operates the procedures for collecting revenues for the Federation. It operates a Planetary Accounting Office. But after the explosion of wealth following the establishment of the constitutional, global civilization, it became not a question of keeping track of the wealth but to monitor its non-stop flow. Once we had wealth like we had air, the whole game of economics was transformed.

7.   Commission for Legislative Review-

It examines legislation to see if any has become obsolete. And with the rapid development of new information, they had a challenge keeping up

with it all. A piece of legislation could actually become obsolete before the writing of it had been completed or before it had been voted on."

Interviewer:

"The more I listen, the more I am awed by the vision and commitment you and the all of the early erastists brought forth. We, who are the benefactors of your efforts, thank you."

The Erastist:

"You are quite welcome. I am so grateful to have been able to physically survive long enough to see it all happen!
        You know when we were discussing life-shaping moments? Well, after you have had one or a number of them, there is no choice but to follow the vision they instill.
        Now comes Article 9, "The World Judiciary". The World Supreme Court and the whole court system on the planet are established. They have jurisdiction, or deciding judgment, in all major cases and litigations. The decisions of the World Supreme Court would be binding on all parties.
        The benches, or divisions, of the World Supreme Court and their jurisdictions are:
        1.   Bench for Human Rights-
        They deal with issues of human rights arising from conflicts with the rights guaranteed by the World Constitution. Their main focus is maintaining the right of each individual on Earth to live a life of birth to
        death creative freedom. That is one of the biggest things we have achieved.
        2.   Bench for Criminal Cases-
        They are to deal with violations of world law. This not only pertains to individuals but also to corporations, groups, associations, and countries. But as wealth increased, as personal freedom increased, and the creation of the society we now have, violations of the law have all but disappeared. The reasons for violating the law have simply disappeared.

3.   Bench for Civil Cases-
They deal with issues of non-criminal lawsuits. In the reality of life, there are situations requiring legal attention. But again, a lot of that has diminished greatly too.

4.   Bench for Constitutional Cases-
They handled issues dealing with the interpretation of the World Constitution. Maybe this series and the upcoming book will aid them in their efforts.

5.   Bench for International Conflicts-
They took care of legal contests arising between countries of the Federation. They were quite busy in the beginning of the constitutional, global civilization. Even though there now existed a legal, political union on the planet, the historical and cultural factors still existed too.

And war was a traditional result to those problems. But the reality of facing the resistance from the whole planet if they started a war, no country dared. They were eventually able to work out an agreeable erastistic solution.

6.   Bench for Public Cases-
They are responsible for handling conflicts between the Federation and national governments, corporations, or individuals that involve world legislation or world law. Basically, they were to insure that all of these groups worked in cooperative unity instead of in the traditional competitive struggle with one another.

7.   Advisory Bench-
They provide opinions upon request on any legal question regarding world law or world legislation. The primary seat, or location, of the World Supreme Court is in the world capitol along with the World Parliament and the World Executive. Continental seats are in the five different continental divisions of the Earth. They are focused on cases concerning human rights, crime, civil and public cases. The World Supreme Court handles the constitutional, planetary, appellate and advisory cases.

A collegium, or panel, of world judges is established by the World Parliament. It has twenty judges. They are nominated by the House of Counsellors and elected by a majority vote of all three houses of the World Parliament. Their term of office is ten years.

There is a Presiding Council of World Judges consisting of a Chief Justice and four Associate Chief Justices. Their term of office is five years.

The Council assigns all world judges to several benches, which annually chooses a presiding judge.

The members of the different benches are renumbered as necessary. Any judge can be removed from office by a two thirds majority of the World Parliament. Each judge is to have at least ten years of juristic experience, be at least thirty years of age, and show visible competence in world law and the humanities. I particularly liked the inclusion of the humanities!

And lastly, there is to be a Superior Tribunal of the World Supreme Court. It is to handle cases of extraordinary public importance. Any person or group is free to submit cases for their consideration."

Interviewer:

"It seems that all great civilizations throughout history have created detailed judiciary systems as you described.

What else do we look at?"

The Erastist:

"The subject of Article 10 is the "Enforcement System". This enforcement of world law applies directly to the individual who is held responsible for compliance. When world law is violated, the Enforcement System operates to identify and apprehend the responsible individual or individuals.

The enforcement action will not violate the rights of the individual as guaranteed by the World Constitution. The agents of the Enforcement System are equipped with only the appropriate weapons needed.

The Enforcement System is to be headed by an Office of World Attorneys General and a Commission of Regional World Attorneys. The Office is comprised of five members with one being named the World Attorney General and the remaining four as Associates. The World Attorney General office rotates among all five members. The Commission consists of twenty regional attorneys. The members of the Office serve a ten-year term and the Regional Attorneys serve a term of five years.

The World Police are responsible for the apprehension and the arrest of violators of world law. Each regional staff of the World Police is headed by a Captain appointed by the Regional World Attorney. A World Police Supervisor handles activities which transcend regional boundaries. Searches and arrests can only be made with warrants from the Office. They too are armed only with the appropriate weapons. The World Police Captain and the Supervisor serve a ten-year term or can be removed for just cause. But again, I'd like to repeat that as our civilization progressed and crime withered, the World Police became mostly helping to manage salvation and rescue situations."

Interviewer:

"I suppose any social system needs enforcement of the laws. But yes, as wealth increased and our new, global community became less and less of a daily struggle to survive, the crime rates plummeted. There is always that element of criminal thinking in any social system."

The Erastist:

"Yes, that is true. However, we did need a codified system of law to keep the would-be criminals and power-hungry politicians in order. Once we moved from capitalism to democratic socialism, things got much better as you observed. Let us go on with describing that system as it is laid out in the World Constitution.

Article 11 covers the "World Ombudsmus". This is the office of public defender. It is designed to protect the people of the Earth against violations of universal human rights as guaranteed by the World Constitution. They are to press for the implementation of the Direct Principles as defined in Article 13, which I will cover later right around the corner. The office is to keep alert for any perils to humanity arising from new technology and will also receive complaints from any person or group in the Federation.

They are to request the World Attorneys to initiate legal actions whenever considered necessary. The Ombudsmus is to monitor the various departments of the World Government to make sure they are adequately fulfilling their purposes. They are also to present an annual report to the Presidium on the Ombudsmus' activities with recommendations of legislative actions.

The Ombudsmus consists of a council of five members who serve a term of ten years with two possible consecutive terms. A Principle World Ombudsmus is selected to serve two years and then the office rotates to another member of the council. There is another council of twenty members to assist the Principle Ombudmus. These members serve a term of five years with the possibility of four more consecutive terms.

The regional offices are headed by a World Advocate. Any member can be removed for just cause. Members of the World Ombudsmus are to be at least thirty years of age and have at least five years' experience and education in world law."

Interviewer:

"I just love the detailed structure of this Constitution, but I suppose if a world order is to be created, it will necessarily have to be this detailed.

Now, what about Article 12?"

The Erastist:

"Article 12 is a good example of the detail you mention. It is the "Bill of Rights for the Citizens of Earth". It says that equal rights for all citizens of the Federation shall be granted with no discrimination on any grounds. Equal protection and application of world legislation is granted to all of the Federation's citizens, to every human on the planet.

We are granted freedom of speech in all forms except for incitement to violence. Freedom of assembly is granted for peaceful demonstrations. The freedom to vote is assured without censorship or recrimination. Freedom of religion is the right of everyone. Freedom to express political beliefs, not including violence, is guaranteed. Freedom of research and travel are insured.

No one may be arbitrarily arrested without the proper warrant and there is a prohibition against physical and psychological harm. The rights of habeas corpus, or due process of trial, as well as legal protection against ex-post facto laws (things made illegal after someone has done them), double jeopardy, or being tried twice for the same violation, and self-incrimination are guaranteed.

There is a safety of private property from arbitrary seizure without reasonable compensation. Everyone has the right to family planning and free public assistance to achieve family objectives. Everyone has the right to family privacy against surveillance as a means of political control."

Interviewer:

"I always thought that the American Constitution's inclusion of a Bill of Rights was one of the wisest things ever printed by the human race. You've already mentioned Article 13. I guess we are going to cover that now?"

The Erastist:

"Yes. Here is Article 13. It is called the "Directive Principles for the Earth Federation". These are other rights to be guaranteed by the Federation but not specifically listed in the World Constitution. First of these rights is to secure useful employment with suitable wages for everyone. But after we had achieved Fuller's cyborg assistants, this was transformed from finding useful employment to assisting everyone to do what they wanted, having been freed by cybernetic technology.

Citizens of the Federation are to have free public health services and medical care throughout their lives. Also, they are to have equal opportunity for leisure time, but after the cybernetic liberation of everyone, all of everyone's time was leisure time and for their whole lives.

They are to enjoy the benefits of scientific and technological discoveries. They are to have protection from any perils presented by these technological innovations. This included protection of the natural environment too, so that future generations would be able to continue to enjoy this life on Earth as well."

Interviewer:

"I really do get wrapped up in hearing you share this about the World Constitution. The more I hear, the more it sounds like a recipe for a global, excuse me, for a constitutional, global civilization.

Okay, lay Article 14 on us."

The Erastist:

"Article 14 is called "Safeguards and Reservations". One safeguard is to guarantee a full faith and credit to public acts, legislation, and judicial proceedings. Everything would be available to the people. The member countries of the Federation would be assured they would determine their internal political, economic, and social systems being consistent with the World Constitution. The powers not delegated to the Federation by the World Constitution are reserved to the member countries and ultimately to all of the citizens of the Earth Federation."

Interviewer:

"I am sure this appealed to the member countries quite a lot. It made room for different cultural expressions of common law, for the World Constitution."

The Erastist:

"I love your responses! Yes, it is fun to travel to the various member countries and experience their cultural expressions of common law, as you put it. One people on one planet!

Article 15 is "World Federal Zones and World Capitals". There are to be twenty World Federal Zones within the twenty Electoral and Administrative Regions. They serve as locations for the several organs of the Federation. Five World Capitals are to be established in the five Continental Divisions.

One will be designated as the Primary World Capital with the remaining four as Secondary Capitals. The primary organs of the Federation will be in the Primary World Capital with the other organs of the government in the Secondary Capitals. Sessions can be rotated among the capitals as decided by the World Parliament.

Article 16 is "World Territories and Exterior Relations".

In the final Constitution that was ratified, the oceans, atmosphere, satellites, including the moon and the whole solar system, and all of the land were under the jurisdiction of the Federation. There were no world territories or external relations."

Interviewer:

"I can see how the constitutional, global civilization would make some parts of this Constitution obsolete. But it is still a superb document of tremendous historical importance. It is a magnificent foundation to build upon as our knowledge increases."

The Erastist:

"Yes, I'll talk about that more when we reach the section on Amendments. Now, I want to cover Article 17 about the "Ratification and Implementation of the World Constitution".

The article begins with the idea that the World Constitution be transmitted from the United Nations, to all the people on the planet for their ratification. Ratification by the people would be decided by a simple majority vote. That vote would be ratified by the national legislatures and, in turn, would be ratified by the World Parliament.

But ultimate ratification would be based on the majority vote of the people on the planet. Voting is by citizens with bodies eighteen years of age or older. Once ratified, the member countries would then be bound by law NEVER to have armed conflict with any other member country.

If any member country did start a war, it would be considered an attack on all the countries of the whole Federation and would be responded to as the global threat it is. This was soon followed by full disarmament, and the World Constitution became the supreme law of planet Earth. I'd like to add here that the citizens of the planet voted nearly 100% in favor of this Constitution.

The implementation of the World Constitution will be done in three stages: The First Operative Stage, The Second Operative Stage, and The Full Operative Stage."

Interviewer:

"That sounds simple enough. If the planet is to be made into one homogenous, political entity, into one country, then it is a matter of the majority of citizens wanting and voting for its creation. Then, it is only a matter of constructing the global civilization that's laid down in the World Constitution."

The Erastist:

"Exactly! The erastists, who brought the constitutional, global civilization into existence, thought the exact same thing. Sounds like you would have been with us from day one! Each of the member countries came into being that way. What was a matter then of national unification now had become a matter of global unification. One People on One Planet!

126

Now, Article 18 is "Amendments". Like the earlier national constitutions allowed for an amendment process, so does the World Constitution. Amendments can be proposed by a simple majority of the World Parliament or by the people themselves through petitions signed by at least 200,000 voters.

An amendment from the people is proposed if it gets a simple majority vote in the House of the Peoples. Passage is by a two-thirds majority in each of the three Houses of the World Parliament.

Lastly, there is Article 19, "Actions to Be Taken by the World Constituent Assembly". Its first action was to issue the World Constitution to the entire planet for ratification. It is also to establish the following commissions:

1.   Ratification
2.   World Elections
3.   World Development
4.   World Disarmament
5.   World Problems-
This also includes a special commission for the world's worst problems like hunger poverty, pollution, and war.
6.   Nominating
7.   Finance
8.   Peace Research and Education
9.   Any other commission deemed necessary

There are more aspects outlined in Article 19 that I have covered already.

But finally, we had the recipe for a constitutional, global civilization! I am so pleased to have been able to contribute to its creation, along with the billions of other erastists all around the world."

Interviewer:

"Your recall of such a complex document is impressive!" Well, this concludes this episode, my friends. I hope you, our listeners, enjoyed it as

127

much as we have bringing it to you. So, please join us again next week when we spend some more time with The Erastist. See you then! Good night!"

EPISODE SIX

CREATING THE CONSTITUTIONAL, GLOBAL CIVILIZATION

Interviewer:

"What about your tours to reach the planet with the new World Constitution and the actual creation of our constitutional, global civilization?"

The Erastist:

"After I left The Shoes, I first began by performing for various political demonstrations, for the Unitarian Universalist, Presbyterian, and Unity churches, and for numerous universities around the United States. The churches proved to be fertile ground for erasism. They were already centered on the idea of us being one people on one planet.

The offering of the creation of a constitutional, global civilization fell on many eager ears and hearts. They started doing their part by organizing their other church members around the world to back the creation of the constitutional, global civilization. They were often the leaders of the later marches calling for its creation.

The political demonstrations were equally fruitful. The first one was an anti-Klu Klux Klan protest. It seems that several left-wing groups were planning to hold a march in North Carolina, and they contacted the Klan and dared them to try to do anything to stop it. Well, some of the Klan responded by coming to the march and shooting six of the participants to death. I was invited to perform for an anti-Klan rally that was at the end of a second march held in memory of the murdered members.

There were about 7,000 people in attendance and a stage full of presenters and performers. The stage director said we each had only five minutes and we would be escorted off the stage if we went over that limit. The song I was going to perform was about five minutes long, but it worked out fine, right on time.

Right before I was to perform, they introduced members of the slain victims' families. They and the organizers worked the audience into a frenzy, and then I was introduced to the cries of 7,000 people chanting "Death to the Klan, Death to the Klan!"

My song was one I had written as a tribute to Martin Luther King, Jr., so I just said: "If you really want to change things, pay attention to

130

Martin Luther King." One of the things I personally remember was my ex-wife, Lee, who had accompanied me to the show, dancing enthusiastically, excitedly beside the stage in the audience and clapping their hands while I sang.

When I finished the song, one of the stagehands asked me where did I get that song? I said, "I wrote it." I was then approached by some members of the press and was also interviewed on a radio program. And that was the beginning of everything that has brought me here tonight.

Next, I performed at an anti-draft march in Washington, D.C. There were lots of sympathetic ears for a constitutional, global civilization that would bring an end to war. There were about 5,000 at that event. I forget now the song I did. Isn't that odd? I'm sure it had an erastistic message. But I got more press coverage from being there too.

The universities were equally fertile ground for erasism. There were already many collegiate organizations focused on the environment, political issues, and social inequities. I played campuses from the Atlantic to the Pacific, from the Canadian border to the Rio Grande, and even in Canada and Alaska. I received numerous acknowledgements from the people who booked me, which I could use for further appearances.

One thing I could include in the university events was a workshop. In it, we covered the Einstein/Fuller information explosion to show its effects on physics, biological identification, scarcity economics, and nation-based politics. Basically, it showed how our traditional systems in these areas were now obsolete, as we all now know.

Again, Einstein showed the Universe is not just a collection of things in space, but it is doing something. The energy being released is being transformed into life and the ultimate expression of this life is human beings, the creative, intelligent, energy beings in the Universe. And we, on this planet, are only local examples of that general phenomenon. Synergetics!

We were taught we are our bodies. We became trapped in the ideas we belong to some sub-human identity based on biological differences like skin color. We were taught we are male or female, young or old. And our lives were passed inside this cage.

I got into reading a lot of Kurt Vonnegut too. He wrote a short story called <u>Unready to Wear.</u> In it, the main character learns how to separate themselves, the creative, intelligent energy, from their body. Then, they were free to fly around the world, and even the Universe, and see things. The main character then taught the rest of the others in their town to be able to do that too. And they taught others. Soon, everyone came to enjoy living like that rather than in their bodies.]

So, they built a huge mausoleums to store their bodies in and lived their new, joyous existence. Whenever they wanted to do something physical, they would select a body, any body, in one of the mausoleums, and do whatever they wanted to do physically. Sometimes, they would hold big parades and be different people in them. For one parade, they might be a bystander. For another, they could be the King or Queen of the parade. We are energy beings! It's like Jesus said: I'm one and you're one too. I also liked Yoda from the Star Wars movies saying, "Luminous beings are we, not this crude matter."

We were taught that we are in a reality of competition with everyone else over scarce resources that make some people rich and a lot of people poor. We saw billions of humans living in squalor and under fed if fed at all. We saw the planet being torn apart to fuel what was being called progress.

We were taught we only lived on an artificial piece of the planet, in artificial political units called countries. And we could resort to war to solve any disagreements we might have with one another. And these "countries" had various kinds of laws. They could, and would, concentrate all political power into a few people and the rest of the population had to go along with their laws or be brutally punished by torture and/or execution. And all of this was only traditional fables. It was not true!

It was then I moved into covering the World Energy Network and the constitutional, global civilization. The students ate it up. It gave them an attainable vision of a bright future for themselves and for their offspring. This all resulted in the formation of campus organizations everywhere. Like with the churches, they networked with other universities all over the world and focused on spreading erasism. They were the primary organizers of a lot of the demonstrations I'll mention later.

I mentioned that I attended some transformational seminars created by Werner Erhard that basically freed my thinking. The thinking I have now! They showed that the Mind is the psychological repository of the make-up of the culture we are born into and our experiences in that culture. Its main function is to keep us safe in that culture. It talks to us non-stop. It tries to be dominant over the creative, intelligent energy being that was born here.

The Mind is like a radio broadcasting 24 hours a day and 7 days a week. At night, it dreams. In the day, it yaks and yaks. My Mind started when I was three years old when I had an experience based on sex and sex ruled a great deal of my life for a long, long time. Now, it has become something I have experienced, have no more use for, and have learned to ignore the Mind's incessant talking about sex or any other thing that it might want to use to control me. The trick is to dismiss the thought as soon as it occurs. I created a few mental ways if dismissing any unwanted thought.

I got to thinking once about how many Me's there in my Mind. There is the me that is here right now, and there is the me recording in the studio, the me performing my music in concerts, the me giving presentations to world leaders and average citizens as well, the me that is the songwriter and the me that is the author and video maker, the me that lifts weights, the me in my family, and me the erastist and the real me, the creative energy being, that has the Mind.

I thought once the Mind is like the fuel injector in a car engine. It wants to interject the negative fuel from the traditions in which we were raised in and our experiences in that culture into our thinking and moods. But we, the humans of creative, intelligent energy, have our own culture and new traditions. And our foot controls the fuel injector! We control what fuel is fed to the engine of our thinking. We can feed the positive fuel of creative intelligence, happiness, and joy instead of the archaic, negative fuel from the Mind based on fear.

But most of the time, we just need to tell the Mind to shut up. There were things in my past that the Mind wanted to torture me with. A great deal of my time was spent in overcoming the plagues of thinking that my Mind wanted to beat me up with. I think I said before the Mind makes a good servant but a poor master. I eventually cited the title to an old rock'n'roll Chuck Berry song, "Hit the Road, Jack!" I had no time to listen.

There was no space for these thoughts to dwell in. The Mindis incessant but we have to decide if we are going to listen or not.

I met someone in those seminars I mentioned who told me of a guy in the seminar system who had recently been to Russia. I contacted the guy and they told me about their contact in Russia, who of course turned out to be Semyonovich Pushkin. I contacted Semyonovich and they, in very competent English, said they would be delighted to have me come to Russia, stay with them, and we could perform together.

So, I started to do some fundraising shows to pay for the trip. I did several shows at a small pub where I had played with The Shoes. Donna, my second wife, my friend, Dave, and I played there some too. My friends and family filled the place completely.

They were really exciting nights. I also got some media coverage about the trip. There were a couple of newspaper stories too with pictures. I I was invited to be on a popular radio show, be interviewed about the trip and the creation of the constitutional, global civilization.

Then it came time to leave. I flew from home to Atlanta, Georgia. That seemed to be the departure point for trips to Europe and beyond. From Atlanta, I flew to Frankfurt, Germany. I couldn't believe I was actually in the birthplace of my family! The next day, I flew to Moscow.

There I connected with Semyonovich and we headed off into Moscow. When I returned home, I just flew the same route in reverse.

When I went to Russia, it was during the flowering of perestroika and glasnost. These are terms that Mikhail Gorbachev, as the new Secretary General, coined to provide an idea of how he planned to transform the Soviet Union.

"Perestroika" roughly translates as reconstruction. And that is exactly what Gorbachev wanted to do, reconstruct the Soviet Union. "Glasnost" is freedom of speech. Providing that one freedom would itself have revolutionized Soviet society. In fact, it did. In 1991, the member states of the Soviet Union declared their independence and the Soviet Union ceased to exist.

Thanks to Semyonovich, I did five shows there, had the freedom to share my eracistic philosophy, and had the opportunity to meet several really good musicians. One I had the good fortune to meet was Nikita Chekov, a musician and producer of the biggest concerts I did there. They were producing a three-day bluegrass concert at the time of my tour there. Semyonovich got to speak to Nikita after our audition performance, and we were on the show.

As we all now know, this coincidence was another example of God remaining anonymous. I was the only one from the United States on the bill and, being from Kentucky, both the Russian bluegrass musicians and audience thought I was wonderful.

There was a reception for all the people connected to the concert held at the Armand Hammer Hotel. This show was called The Farmers' Concert. It was designed to raise support for the Russian farmers like Willie Nelson's Farm-Aid Concerts did for the American farmers. There I was met by the media too. They were crucial in getting the word out to a much wider audience.

The stage for the concert was huge. There were some very good musicians there. I really enjoyed the backstage warm ups. It certainly got everyone in the groove, and all I needed was to get on stage. I played for I forget how long. My finale was a medley of the first verse of "Amazing Grace" and the whole of "Will the Circle Be Unbroken". When I started "Amazing Grace", five of the Russian musicians jumped on stage and sang it with me, in English!

For the finale, there was Nikita with his red guitar and two female singers from two of the other groups. One of them, Olga, was the hostess of the concert. They had started their own bluegrass group and called it Redgrass. At the time they named the group, the country was still known as the Soviet Union whose flag was red; the name had a humorous twist. Gregori, a banjo player from the Small Town Band, my host, Semyonovich on guitar and harmonica, and Boris on flute rounded out one of the best bands I have ever played with.

That was a life shaping moment too. There were no members of different sovereign countries on stage. There were no different races on stage. There were no different genders on stage. There were no different ages on stage. There were only some human beings on stage doing what human beings are supposed to be doing: having fun and being creative, in this instance, by playing music. It was an actual experience that my life's work has been all about and, like the old song goes, how are you going to keep someone "down on the farm after they have seen gay Paree?"!

After that, the experience continued at the Soviet-American Citizens Summit II. Once again, there were only everyday humans meeting other everyday humans and discussing some everyday things in addition to the major problems facing both of them. Same thing at the concert I did in Dubna, south of Moscow, for the families of the workers at the Soviet Nuclear Research Center. I'm pretty sure I was performing in the home of the Russian atomic bomb.

All around Moscow, there are halls dedicated to different groups. Semyonovich was fortunate enough to get us a booking to perform in the House of Artists. The music went over very well, but really I wondered how many could understand the words.

I then appeared on a national television show that aired to 100 million viewers across 11 time zones. In fact, the show had been on the air for over 26 years, and my performance was the first, and as far as I know, the only episode, to have been repeated. I don't know if this is accurate or not, but my understanding is, it was repeated more than once too.

Here is a song I wrote as a tribute to John Lennon that I did on the show:

For John Lennon

I

John, this song
Is for you
You're the one
Who brought it through
As I stood
And watched you play
Said, that's going to be
Us someday

II

Time has come
To say it again
To survive
We gotta be friends
This whole thing
Could go sour
This could be
Our final hour

Chorus:

We are all family
Part of you
Is part of me
There is nothing
We cannot do
Share the world
Believe that it's true

III

There's a spirit

137

That is you
Don't let no one
Steal your cool
Do what you can
To be free
Be you
And I'll be me"

Interviewer:

"Everyone I know shares the same sentiments as you express in that song! I really liked the cut you have on your first CD, <u>The Solar Age</u>. I think John would have liked it too."

The Erastist:

"Yes, that song was a real ice breaker. It led to that recording session where I had a great time performing the song again with some top notched musicians. And another thing, Semyonovich knew some excellent photographers and I got lots of really nice photos to use later. They got some great shots of me performing at the Farmer's Concert.

One of the more impressive things I saw while in Russia was Red Square. The thing that caught my attention was the Soviet flags flying from atop the Kremlin. I grew up seeing the United States flags at government buildings. It was just visually different.

And St. Basil's Cathedral was magnificent. I have always been awed by the ability of humanity to construct such artistically magnificent structures with the technology at their disposal at the time. The power of human creativity is truly awesome.

After the Russian tour, I did a return tour in Western Europe. I started off at the Unity church in Birmingham, England. I had been a member of the choir at a Unity church in my hometown. Through my hometown church, I was able to set up several events at Unity churches around the world. And I was able to stay with some wonderful Servas hosts too.

Then it was time to return to Germany. My Servas hosts there were great. One I stayed with was a college professor who had a decent command of English. One day, they took me on a tour of their city, Mainz, and we spoke German the whole time. They showed me some Roman ruins, including a tower that the people had built, and my host showed me a number of churches from different periods of history.

When we got back to their home, they told their wife, who did not speak English, that I could speak German. While my host was at work, the wife and I had some good conversations. I am always amazed how humans are the same everywhere. Different expressions of that common creative intelligence.

Next came Austria. I went to a small city south of Vienna called Lafnitz to stay with Wolfgang, a Servas host there. I performed at an Irish-styled pub. The owner had been to Ireland and really was taken by the pubs, so upon their return, they opened probably the only "Irish" pub in Austria. Then I did go to Vienna and stayed with Servas hosts there too. In one place, I was given a bed that was sitting in a loft about two meters off the floor. And of course, the architecture in Vienna, especially the cathedrals, was stupefying.

Then it was on to Switzerland. I stayed in Zurich with Rene and Ursula, you guessed it, Servas hosts. I was given a private room with a bed that looked as if it was made for a honeymoon night. As it turned out, there was a city fair being held the next day. It was only held every four years, and I was fortunate enough to be there when it was. As I walked along the boardwalk where the fair was being held and was greeted by numerous music sites playing a wide variety of music styles. I even heard bluegrass and country music.

When I got back home from Europe, I headed for Australia and New Zealand. I started off in Sydney. I did some shows and again, stayed with Servas hosts. I have done all of this traveling without paying anything for room and board. I took a boat tour around Sydney harbor and got to see the Sydney Opera House and several other very unique sites. After I sent

Marie a picture of me on the boat with the opera house behind me, they sent one back with their name sprayed painted on the opera house. It was quite amusing!

From Sydney, I went to Melbourne and stayed with Loryn and their husband, also Servas hosts! And I also met a guy who lived in a geodesic home! This is a dome structure developed by Buckminster Fuller. It was the first Fuller home I had the pleasure of staying in.

We played a game of Scrabble. Loryn's husband was a computer programmer, and I told them I once heard that computer programmers sometimes just put things in a computer to frustrate us. They slyly smiled and said: "Some people think so."

In New Zealand, I stayed partly with a Unitarian family. The Unitarians say they are the place where religion and reason meet. They say that

as human beings, we are by our nature on a spiritual journey. They say the religious denomination, if we have one, is irrelevant basically. We, as humans, are on the same spiritual journey. That's important and says we all are on one people on one planet.

I rented a car and drove the highway that circles New Zealand's South Island and got to see some wonderful sights. There were numbers of places to pull off the road and look at the countryside. No matter where you travel on the planet, there is always beautiful scenery to enjoy. The Earth is so pretty!

As I mentioned earlier, after returning from Russia, I went on a tour with two of the Russians I had met while in Moscow: Semyonavich, my host there, and Boris, the superb flutist. We toured the state of Florida and did some shows in other places. It only served to support my vision of using music to shift the thinking of the people of Earth to a planetary consciousness."

Interviewer:

"I think it sounds like a marvelous experience! And the Servas organization sounds marvelous too! Tell us more about you living your dream adventures."

The Erastist:

"Yes, it has been a lifelong, dream adventure!

Well next, it was time for a global tour. Wayne and Everett were not in a position to make such a tour. So, I went solo as I had been doing. I began rehearsing for a world tour featuring me and maybe later local musicians from the places I would be playing. Brian, my booking agent, spent hours, days, and weeks setting up the tour. It was very gratifying to hear musicians from all over the world playing my music and the audiences singing the songs along in English.

To begin the tour, I began with a spring concert in New York City's Central Park. It was attended by over 100,000 people. Besides me, there were a number of other famous musicians also participating. Some of them had even autographed my guitar. This made for a superb media event and all of the major news networks were there. That laid the groundwork for the news media all around the world to be waiting for me when I arrived to perform in their backyard.

Next, I headed to Ireland. My shows there included both the northern and southern halves of the island. The shows opened up the space that soon resulted in the unification of the island. Then, I went to England. In honor of The Beatles, I began in Liverpool where they had begun their journey. Then it was down the west coast into Wales, across to London, and then up the east coast to Scotland.

From there, it was only a hop to Sweden, Norway and Finland. The people there were ahead of most people on the planet in having a global consciousness. They were generally considered the happiest people on the planet. Of course, my ideas of creating a global version of what they had created fell on very receptive ears.

Another hop and I was in Denmark and down into Germany. Remember I used to teach German and I was able to talk to the audiences in a common language. Needless to say, I was very well received. In all of these places, the people were already very erastistic in their thinking.

Then I headed east to Poland and got to see first-hand the Nazi death camps. Why that wasn't enough to get a constitutional, global civilization created I'll never know. There was a big movement calling for a constitutional, global civilization after WWII, but the Cold War ended that until the erastists arrived. After that, I headed to Austria, where I got another chance to use my German.

The Czech Republic and Romania were next, down into Greece and over to Italy, through the Alps into France, Belgium and the Netherlands. From there, I headed back to France and into Spain and Portugal. I crossed over the Straits of Gibraltar and into Morocco, North Africa. While in Africa, I was awed by the size of the Sahara. I thought what a solar resource for electrical energy it could be.

Then I traveled down the west coast of the African continent. From Morocco, I headed south to Mali. I played in the capital cities of each "country". Next, I performed in Nigeria. I really enjoyed that show. I was very well received. Then I travelled over to The Republic of Congo. In my childhood, when I wanted to live like Tarzan, I thought of going to the Congo or Madagascar as places where I could do that.

From the Congo, I headed to South Africa, the land of Nelson Mandela, who always had been a hero and an inspiration for me. I always wished I could have met them. I always had a yen to go to South Africa and here I was where Nelson actually had lived.

From the Horn of Africa, I headed north again along the east coast of the continent to Tanzania. I had grown up and lived my life watching shows about nature. A good deal of the time, they focused on the wildlife of Africa. A lot of those shows were made in Tanzania. But again, the time constraints of tour had me committed to very brief interaction with the places where I was appearing.

Next on the list was Ethiopia, one of the oldest "countries" on the planet. As a history teacher, I was fairly familiar that it certainly had a tumultuous history, and human history itself is bound hand in hand with Ethiopia's history.

And then it was on to Egypt. The pyramids were amazing. I thought they proved people could do anything they set their minds to. I think they could have handled building the World Energy Network if they had the technology back then.

From there, I entered the Middle Eastern countries. My concerts were very well-attended because of the contacts I had made with the Nation of Islam thanks to Muhammed Ali. I went into Saudi Arabia first and then turned north to Israel, Turkey and Afghanistan.

Then, I jumped up to Moscow and got to visit with some old friends I had met when I was there with Semyonovich. Then I jumped again to Pakistan, to India and then headed to Southeast Asia. That took me once more down to Australia and New Zealand and then back up to China, the Korean Peninsula and Japan. I must admit it was humbling to see so many people. I really got a grasp of the enormity of my undertaking.

Next, I flew from Japan to Hawaii and then to Alaska. I travelled down the west coast of Alaska through western Canada and into the states of Washington, Oregon, California, New Mexico, Arizona and then into Mexico. From there, I headed down through Central America. Many of these "countries" suffered from some pretty brutal national governments. They were eager to hear about a global society where they would not be abused. Sort of a global perestroika.

From Mexico, I went down the west coast through Belize and into Guatemala and had a great show there. Then I travelled through El Salvador into Honduras with other great events there. Next came Nicaragua with another receptive audience. I had the same experiences in Costa Rica and Panama. Everywhere I met thousands of avid erastists in support of the constitutional, global civilization.

And then I went into South America. From Panama, I travelled right into Columbia with a continuation of the acceptances I got in Central America. I turned west and went through Ecuador to reach Peru. I really wanted to see Machu Picchu. How they were able to construct such magnificence in such an unbelievable place was very impressive. After Peru, it was on into Bolivia, Paraguay, and Argentina for more great audiences and support for the work.

In Argentina, I had reached the southernmost tip of the continent, so I headed north and up the eastern side of South America. I travelled through Uruguay to reach Brazil. I believe Brazil was about the size of the United States, but it was amazing how big it is. I did a couple of shows there. The Amazon Rainforest is unbelievably beautiful. I got a first-hand experience of what we were working to save.

Finally, I went through French Guinea, Suriname, and Guyana to get to Venezuela. After another gratifying experience there, I returned to Columbia where I did another rewarding concert. That led me to travel up the east coast of Central America with even bigger shows since I had already performed in those "countries". Again, any place I did not actually appear was reached via television, radio, movies, cell phones and computers.

I reentered into the United States at the eastern side of Texas and toured across the Deep South. I played in some excellent venues and had some very receptive audiences. I even had the pleasure of sharing a stage with Marie, the mother of my music and who got me started into music in the first place. That alone was a life-shaping moment and a life-long desire!

Then, it was turning north to play along the Atlantic seaboard into Canada. The show we did there was on the eastern side of Canada and televised across the whole nation. From there, I ended up with another concert in New York's Central Park. I think there was close to a million people at that one.

Of course, I was swarmed by the media everywhere, but that only served to be free advertisement of the work and allowed millions of other people on the planet to experience the shows even though they could not be there in person. They not only televised the concerts, but I gave numerous interviews about creating a constitutional, global civilization and the World Energy Network as the means to achieve that. The whole tour lasted three years.

I would like to add a song that, for me, is about the World Energy Network and the creation of the constitutional, global civilization. When I was visiting Paul in San Diego, they had a video screen with Fuller's dymaxion map on it. Superimposed on the map was a grid system showing the flow of electric energy from the World Energy Network around the planet. To me, it looked like a big river system.

Here's the song I wrote, " River of Power:"

River of Power

I

River of Power
Roll on free
Build a new world
For humanity
River of power
Roll on free
River of power
For you and me

II

Power from the sun
All around the Earth
Gridded together
For our rebirth
River of power
Roll on free
River of power
For you and me

Chorus:

End of hunger, war,
And climate change
One world country
We have begun again
River of power
Take us from
Where we have been
River of power
We have begun again.

River of power
Bathe us in purity
Let the past fade
Into obscurity
River of power
Roll on free
River of power
For you and me

I could elaborate on the lyrics, but I think they are self-explanatory."

Interviewer:

"Yes, I think so too. I have always liked that song. You're right, it says the message clearly. And, I did see some of the concerts at the time and admired your commitment and dedication to your vision of a new reality for the planet.

After the tours, what happened?"

The Erastist:

"Yes, I have always been committed to the creation of the constitutional, global civilization. Just as the Founding Fathers in America transformed 13 disunited colonies into a constitutional, national civilization, I saw I was in the historical period of history to transform the hundreds of disunited "countries" into a constitutional, global civilization. So I said I would do what I could.
During the touring of the planet, I made contact with several, local groups who were ideologically in agreement with the creation of the constitutional, global civilization. I used the concerts to direct everyone's attention to these groups and to join in our common, global efforts. This

interconnected billions of people around the planet into one network that I'll mention in a minute.

We found out where the day begins on the planet. I don't know why that spot was chosen as the beginning of the day, but we decided to begin there. We decided to have a series of marches and events in support of the World Energy Network and the establishment of the new civilization. We chose 12:00 noon as the time to begin the march on that spot. As the Earth rotated and it became 12:00 noon in the next time zone on the planet, then the people there held their marches and events.

The outpouring of people around the world was staggering. Countless billions filled major cities, towns, and villages around the world. Of course, the news people were there in force and helped to reach countless other billions with the vision of the World Energy Network and the constitutional, global civilization.

And the message was not lost on the political communities of the planet either. The very next day after the marches and events, I was called and asked to address the United Nations' General Assembly among other organizations and groups. I have already spoken some about this talk. I walked into a tumultuous reception with a standing ovation that lasted 10 minutes. And as I delivered my address, I was met with more standing ovations.

The delegates commonly agreed to present the creation of a constitutional, global government to the leaders of the planet's "countries" that they represented. I took along Glen Martin from the Planetary Constitution Association. Remember, their organization had drafted The Constitution for the Federation of the Earth, which I covered in the last episode and had been working on getting it ratified.

All of this set up the creation of another talk to the leaders of the member "countries" at the United Nations. This second address was extremely well-received. These leaders had all witnessed the marches in their backyards. A committee was set up to draft a final version of the Constitution that would include things various leaders wanted included. Glen had been registering people around the world as world citizens and stored their information into a very good computer system.

Now, Glen was rewarded with billions of people now registering, so that when it came time to ratify the Constitution itself, we had the system

147

ready to let the people of the planet decide. And they did---overwhelmingly! The creation of the constitutional, global civilization was a reality!! Nearly 100% of the people voted to ratify the Constitution.

And all the while, the World Energy Network was being brought online. The decision to begin that was made soon after the talk to the national heads of state at the U.N. And everywhere the Network reached, the results were the same. Hunger disappeared, poverty disappeared, pollution disappeared, and war disappeared. Not overnight to be sure but pretty quickly, and everyone saw the beginning of the end of these plagues that people had suffered from the beginning of human history.

But, finally, we had the constitutional, global civilization! I am so pleased to have been able to contribute to its creation, along with the billions of other erastists all around the world. One thing I have always relished is, that after the World Constitution was ratified, they called that day "Erasism Day".

I'd like to conclude this series with a song that has become an anthem for our constitutional, global civilization.

It's called "The One World Song":

The One World Song

I

The highways of history
Have brought us here
Away from the past
Away from all fear
Highways of history
Keep us rolling along
'Til we learn to sing
The one world song!

Chorus:

The one world song!

The one world song!
'Til we learn to sing
The one world song!

II

The highways of history
Have made us one
On our own path
No race to be won
Highways of history
Keep us rolling along
'Til we learn to sing
The one world song!

Chorus:"

Interviewer:

"That _is_ a marvelous song!

Well, my friends in TV land, this concludes our series on the story of the Erastist. On behalf of all the viewers, the production staff, and myself, I want to deeply thank you for sharing your story with us.

Your vision inspired countless people all over the planet, our beloved Earth. Your decades of unrelenting commitment gave hope and solutions to the desperate and to the extinction-level threats that faced us all. Your music, books, documentaries, touring, and public speaking were a blessing to us all.

And, of course, thank you for your contributions to the realization, dare I say it, of our beloved constitutional, global civilization!

Please don't forget to watch the documentary on this upcoming Earth Day on this station honoring the life of the one and only: The Erastist!

Good night, everyone and Peace!"

Quotes of The Erastist

1. "There is little possibility that whatever we create will ever be recognized or rewarded, but there is zero possibility if we do not create anything. The joy comes from the creation of what you love and not in the recognition it receives."

2. "Humans are the creative, intelligent energy that gives life to the body. We are the content and the body is the container."

3. "I eventually decided to keep working, especially on music, so even if I were never recognized during my biological time here. I might reincarnate and become a child prodigy like Mozart."

4. "Martin Luther King said, "I have a dream." And don't we all? If what we dream is the reality we have left behind, then we were dreaming the wrong dream. King's dream launched the one we are experiencing now."

5. "I once heard someone describe fuels like coal and oil as fossilized sunlight. That pretty much summed up the concept of energy for me. It showed we have all the energy we will ever need coming in free from our life-giving star now and need not gouge out fossilized sunlight to burn and pollute our air and change the climate."

6. "Ever since the Stone Age, meat was considered a primary source of nutrition and nourishment. But after its connection to serious physical maladies, the aging of the body caused by digesting it, its polluting effects on the environment, and it being a main cause of global starvation were learned, its elimination became a moral issue and brought forth the elimination of its use like other moral issues such as slavery and the like."

151

7. "When I was a kid, I would have loved to have lived in the nineteenth century. I was so steeped in my attraction to Native Americans, I thought that was the time of history for me, the past. But after being introduced to the works of Einstein and Fuller, I came to the realization that the life their discoveries offered meant I was actually trapped in the past. It was now like living when it was learned that the Earth is round and orbiting the sun and nearly everyone else on the planet still thought it was flat with the Universe orbiting it."

8. "Once we realized how much we stood to gain by living as one, human family instead of as sub-human groups imprisoned in obsolete traditions, we began to see the ending of the end of the ills these traditions caused: hunger, poverty, pollution and war."

9. "I watched a show on public television called NOVA. It has been one of my favorites and I usually said that if it was on NOVA, I'd watch it. This episode was on the creation of the Webb Space Telescope. The telescope took nearly 20 years to build and involved thousands of people in the project. The plan was to put the telescope into orbit a million miles from the Earth. It was to focus on the deep, dark depths of space.
They focused on a small piece of dark, seemingly empty, part of space about the diameter of a soda straw. The telescope revealed there were thousands of whole galaxies in that space! A scientist, working on the project, said: "International cooperation is needed to make great things happen." Exactly what I thought concerning the creation of the World Energy Network and the constitutional, global civilization."

10. "It occurred to me one day that listening to the Mind's ceaseless chatter is like watching television. If you don't like what you're hearing, change the channel. Life is great when you are on top of it instead of it being on top of you!"

11. "A friend of mine's son read my books and saw my documentary and really identified with erasism. They were very good in the business world and had travelled around the world. They found that in some areas, people had no access to recycling. Gregor, my friend's son,

decided to do what they can, where they can, when they can, the best they can. They got that, my personal motto, from one of my books!

Gregor raised $100,000 and went to China and made the first kind of recycling machine they wanted. They also made contact with businesspeople in areas without recycling access and created a market for the technology they were offering. That was actually an actual example of the success of my work."

12. "I have a brother from a different mother who is a prolific reader. They told me once of a book that covered the Chaos Theory. The idea is that everyone, by their mere existence, has an impact on the nature of our global reality however miniscule that may be. That impact may never be known by us, but it is there, nonetheless. That is why it's so important to be and do the best we can."

13. "Throughout history, a number of groups have talked about what they called a "holy war". That is the same as talking about a "virgin prostitute". They are mutually contradictive terms! There is nothing holy about any war."

14. "Looking back on the learning experience of songwriting, I am very grateful for having learned how to add beats and chord changes to my lyrics. Before I learned how to do that from a drummer friend, I am sure other musicians thought I was some sort of a musical Picasso in the beginning. I played music but it wasn't as formatted as they were used to. But as we all know now, I did learn."

15. "When the carbon dioxide poisoning of our atmosphere became a crisis that had to be dealt with, it seemed the technology just sprang out of the ground to rid the air of this extinction level threat. Of course, the elimination of the other fossil fuels was primary also in order to clean the air. Technology that allowed certain minerals that absorbed carbon dioxide were developed into bricks that could be buried and hold the gas for at least 1,000 years. Also other substances were developed that absorbed carbon dioxide like a sponge absorbs water. Now it's no longer a threat!"

16. "I was visiting a friend who had worked with me in the early days. We were sitting at a table that had a small picture frame on it leaning against the wall. In the frame were a number of buttons. On one, it said "Eating Meat Is Obsolete". I thought that button was totally charming and said it all!"

17. "I think I have mentioned that the planet Venus once had oceans, but the runaway release of carbon dioxide by volcanic eruptions turned the atmosphere into about 80% carbon dioxide which caused a greenhouse effect to heat the surface of the planet to over 800 degrees.
I had an apartment once on the 8th floor of a high-rise building that overlooked an expressway with 24/7, non-stop traffic on it. I thought to myself, these are our Venus volcanoes. I wrote a song about that but named it Earth Volcanoes. Our mechanical volcanoes were doing to our atmosphere what Venus' volcanoes did to Venus' atmosphere."

18. "I once heard a definition of belief as accepting something as true with no concrete proof. I think a lot of truths we left behind in creating the constitutional, global civilization were like that. What Einstein and Fuller achieved was to establish concrete beliefs based on mathematics.
Like Spinoza once said, God may know much more than we do, but what we know mathematically, we know as well as God does. Mathematics provides what Ray Monk calls "cast-iron foundations" for belief."

19. "Once people realized that they themselves were a part of the solution to the problems that beset everyone, it stimulated a passion to act, a vision to pursue, and revolutionary renovations to create the world we have now. Like a Native American Innuit activist said about their connection to the land, "It gave us resilience". That is what our reborn connection to the planet also instilled in us, resilience."

20. "We happened to have lived at a time when science, theology, and philosophy merged into agreement. Einstein and Fuller scientifically showed, the religious leaders spiritually showed, and philosophers wisely showed we are creative, intelligent energy beings."

21. "I was very appreciative of the highly competent bands that backed me on the world tours. It showed me the music had made a significant impact. But when I saw and heard the audiences singing my songs in English, I knew we had a global movement on our hands. And I was right!"

22. "I saw a show on public television that contained a segment on honoring the women who assumed the jobs in the factories, especially armament ones, during World War II while the men went off to fight the war. They were called Rosie the Riveters. One was interviewed and they said, "We were doing it to save our country."

When people were interviewed after the creation of the constitutional, global civilization and the elimination of hunger, poverty, pollution and war, they often said, "We were doing it to save our planet.""

23. "I learned that at the time the major programs were created to lay the foundation for a pollution-free planet , 48 million tons of plastic were being dumped into the environment every year. 8 million tons of that were dumped into the oceans every year. It was calculated that in 26 years, the plastic would outweigh the fish in the oceans."

24. "I was horrified when I learned about what was being done to females on certain parts of the planet because of obsolete traditions. They were being surgically altered to meet male standards sexual. The females were having their clitorises removed and their vaginas cut and re-sown to fit their husbands' penises. Female infants were having their vaginas surgically stretched so by the age of 2, they could hold a grown man's penis. And all of this with no pain killers! This was another strong incentive for the constitutional, global civilization!"

25. "Songwriting, for me, is like raising children. I suppose all artistic expression is like that. First there is the joy of the conception of the inspirational idea for the song. Like a fertilized egg, it comes to life. The lyrics are the soul of the song, and the music is the life of the song. A fetus comes into being and begins to grow.

Then the song goes through a period of gestation with the beats and chords being smoothed out and the song is born. Like a human child, it

155

goes through its childhood, adolescence and early adult stages. The song enters the studio and becomes a mature adult. From there, it is sent out into the world to see what impact it might have.

I have created about 200 children myself and another 100 with my music mentor, Dave. Some of them are still fetuses, but others have gone out into the world and helped make history beginning with the World Energy Network and the constitutional, global civilization. I was fortunate to have a number of successful music children!"

26. "I turned on the public television station once and there was a series starting that was as if I had written and hosted it. It even had a title nearly identical to the title of my first book. In one episode, the show's creator and host talked about how people answered 'What if' questions. They said usually the answers focus on some disastrous event of one kind or another.

But then the host asked about answering 'What if' questions with positive results like: What if we are successful? What if we do get it right?

What if we do create a future beyond our imaginations? What if we do become great ancestors? It spoke to me deeply.

In that regard, I have always admired Robert F. Kennedy too. I have not forgotten them saying that some people look at things the way they are and ask: Why? Kennedy said they look at things that have never been and ask, "Why not?" That spoke to me deeply too."

27. "I am not a special case person. I have had the blessing to have been able to learn information that opened the door to unbelievable freedoms such as from the creation of the World Energy Network and the constitutional, global civilization."

Bibliography

Einstein, Albert, <u>Out of My Later Years</u>, (New York: Philosophical Library, Inc., 1950)

Einstein, Albert, <u>The World As I See It</u>, (New York: Philosophical Library, Inc., 1949)

Fuller, R. Buckminster, <u>Operating Manual for Spaceship Earth</u>, (New York: Simon & Schuster, 1969)

Fuller, R. Buckminster, <u>Utopia or Oblivion, The Prospects for Humanity</u>, (New York: The Overlook Press, 1969)

Fuller, R. Buckminster, <u>Synergetics, Explorations in the Geometry of Thinking</u>, (New York: MacMillan Publishing Company Incorporated, 1975)

Fuller, R. Buckminster, <u>Earth, Inc.</u> (Garden City, New York: Anchor Press/Doubleday, 1973)

Fuller, R. Buckminster and Marks, Robert, <u>The Dymaxion World of Buckminster Fuller</u>, (New York; Anchor Press, 1973)

The Institute for Economic Democracy, <u>The Constitution for the Federation of the Earth</u>, c. 2016

MICHAEL KESSLER

Michael has spoken and performed his original songs throughout the United States and in England, Germany, Austria, Switzerland, Netherlands, Russia, Australia, and New Zealand presenting his programs on world peace. He has recorded six albums of his original music, written four books, hosted a television series, and produced a fifty minute documentary to present the opportunities and necessities of creating an advanced, environmentally friendly, constitutional, global civilization.